DAD'S Parenting Playbook

The S-M-I-L-E-S Approach to Raising Resilient Kids

William T. Terry MD

©2009 by William T. Terry, MD. All rights reserved.

ISBN: 1-4392-2919-8
ISBN 13: 9781439229194

Visit www.booksurge.com to order additional copies.

TABLE OF CONTENTS

FIRST QUARTER 1

Chapter 1
Where's the Playbook?
The S-M-I-L-E-S Concept of Parenting 3

Chapter 2
Dads and Moms Are Different:
Jumping Out of a Six-Foot Hole 11

Chapter 3
Support:
An Unsupported Child Cannot Survive 21

SECOND QUARTER 33

Chapter 4
Modeling for Imitation:
Monkey See; Monkey Do 35

Chapter 5
Limits:
You Gotta Live Within Them, Can't Live Without Them 47

Chapter 6
Education:
Is It Really That Important? 59

HALFTIME

Chapter 7
You Gotta Be a Guy:
Men and Shopping 77

THIRD QUARTER 79

Chapter 8
Don't Say Diet:
Say Lifestyle Change 81

Chapter 9
Exercise:
An Eight-Letter Word 91

Chapter 10
Failure and a Positive Attitude:
The Capacity to Adapt 101

Chapter 11
Resilience:
Adjusting to Misfortune and Change 113

Chapter 12
Parenting as a Team:
The Game Plan 125

FOURTH QUARTER 141

Chapter 13
When Nothing Works:
Troubleshooting Parenting Practices 143

Chapter 14
Spirituality:
The Importance of Attending Religious Services 161

FIRST QUARTER

"Nothing I've ever done has given me more joys and rewards than being a father to my children." —*Bill Cosby, comedian*[1]

"We spend the first twelve months of our children's lives teaching them to walk and talk and the next twelve years telling them to sit down and shut up!" —*Phyllis Diller, comedienne*[2]

"Never have more children than you have car windows." —*Erma Bombeck, author*[3]

CHAPTER 1

WHERE'S THE PLAYBOOK?
The S-M-I-L-E-S Concept of Parenting

Dear Doc:

We got the kid. Thanks for your help, but where's the playbook?

Dad

There's a lot of excitement and bone-deep terror when you hear the words, "We're pregnant!" Then you wait, while watching your blooming spouse grow with child. "Yeah, I did that. That's part of me in there." The visits to the doctor, birthing classes, and ultrasound photos to e-mail or text to all your friends come next. Nine months seem like an eternity, but after a little morning sickness, everything goes along the same as before. You may find yourself thinking how sweet everything will be with another person in your life. *Nothing's going to change very much. This pregnancy thing is a piece of cake.*

One day, contractions start, but *maybe it's false labor. No, the pains are getting closer together!* Suddenly it's game day, and you're suiting up to play but don't have a clue what to do.

What position am I playing? Coach! Coach, I need the playbook! I don't have a playbook.

What do I do now? How can she be so calm? Didn't we practice? Where's my playbook?

I'm not prepared! Remember, breathe. That's right, breathe! Breathe? Me or her?

Wow, she looks like she's in a lot of pain! What am I supposed to do? YIKES! It's time! The baby's coming!

The birth goes fine in spite of your concerns. Once you get home, there's no sitting on the sidelines. You have to hit the ground running. There's a whirlwind of activity. Where's the playbook? Everybody is feeling overwhelmed, and for a while, this becomes the norm. Now it's up to you and Mom to make this game a winning one. But where do you start?

Most of the guys I talk to about parenting say they don't know where to begin. All of a sudden, they have a baby in their lives and are expected to know everything about raising children. They even have to be instructed on how to hold a baby and feed it. "No, don't squeeze it like you would a football. Cradle it gently in your arms. That's it."

No one ever told you anything about parenting other than your dad taking you aside and in a somber and serious tone saying, "It's your job, Son, to be a good father to this child." He didn't hand you a copy of the *Johnson Family Secrets for Raising Children*, nor did he tell you, "If you have any questions, just call." You got pushed into the cold cruel world of parenting without much guidance and with the expectation that you'll fend for yourself. You struggle, you fall, and hopefully you learn from experience.

All the time you are thinking about the responsibility of having another human being totally dependent on you. You're wondering—*Am I doing the right thing? What if I screw up? Will my kid hate me? Am I going to make the same mistakes my parents did? I want to parent differently, but how can I?*

Dads just don't have any place to turn for help. Guys would not be caught dead in the tire shop waiting room looking at a women's magazine article about parenting—unless of course there was an attractive lady on the front cover and the hint of an article on how you can sexually satisfy your man.

WHERE'S THE PLAYBOOK?

Guys certainly don't get parenting tips on ESPN. I can see it now ...

"Let's switch our remote to George 'Baby Bottom' Blanda, who will be demonstrating ten new ways to make diaper-changing fun and exciting! Can we get a close-up there? Get a 'load' of that wiping technique; truly Olympic quality. Let's see that on instant replay."

Can you imagine a young father with his buddies, watching the football game and discussing the weaning of children off of breast milk and on to solid foods?

"Pass the chips and dip. And you know, guys, Cindy and I have been debating whether or not to start feeding Abby cereal or pureed carrots first. What do you think?"

"Johnny's just starting to walk. Do you think we should take him out of his Pampers and put him in Huggies Pull-Ups? Want another beer?"

"Emily is so fussy at night and we're not getting much sleep. Have any of you guys got any suggestions? Is that pizza still hot?"

If it were the guys' wives, this would be a normal conversation. They would be texting each other, getting suggestions, and calling their moms. If you were to call your father and ask him for advice, he would most likely say, "Talk to your mother."

As guys, we may be turned off by stinky diapers and not knowing how to quiet a crying child, but still we want to be the best fathers we can be to our children. At a loss and seeing nowhere to turn, we stumble through parenthood, hoping for the best and fearing the worst. Where are the parenting classes? What about a training camp for dads?

Well, that's all about to change. This book will be the playbook you never received—your owner's manual for raising your child, Parenting 101, the basics, the fundamentals to help you become a "Gold-Medal" dad. You'll also have your own personal coach, Dr. T, a board-certified child and adolescent psychiatrist, giving you direction and advice. This is not a touchy-feely approach to parenting. We will concentrate on the fundamentals. The great coaches keep it simple to produce winning teams and programs.

Like all good coaches do, we will start off by assessing our strengths and weaknesses. Let's face it; dads are at a disadvantage when it comes to parenting skills. For men, understanding our feelings of inadequacy and discomfort with parenting is essential. Men and women are not the same. They have equally important roles in the process, but those roles are distinctly and rightly different.

To start, we need to understand how men and women differ in their biology, psychology, and socialization. It may be politically incorrect, but it is a biological, psychological, and social fact that men and women are fundamentally different. The differences have a purpose, and for that reason should be celebrated rather than minimized.

The fact that guys appear to be light-years away from moms when it comes to raising children does not diminish their importance. It speaks to their need for understanding and support in the process. This book will help you see how you fit into the parenting team and allow you to work on your weaknesses while emphasizing and supporting your strengths.

Well, it ain't gonna be easy. It will be tough, but you can get through it. Dr. T will be giving you the stripped-down basic course in being a dad. Sometimes it may seem too simple. You may tell yourself, "I know that. This is easy. I need something more." But you have to master the basics before you can get into the big leagues. You can't hit a home run until you learn how to swing the bat. You can't throw a touchdown pass until you learn how to grip the ball. It's like the pitching and catching, blocking and tackling, dribbling and passing, running and kicking that you had to learn before you could play the game. It's called the fundamentals.

Aristotle the Greek, the ancient philosopher, once said, "We are what we repeatedly do. Excellence, then, is not an act, but a habit."

Yeah, yeah, practice makes perfect. We all know that. No, as Green Bay Packers Coach Vince Lombardi said, "Perfect practice makes perfect!"[4] If you use bad techniques, you will ingrain bad habits. If you've established bad habits, you have to work even harder to eliminate them.

> *"Football is blocking and tackling. Everything else is mythology." —***Vince Lombardi**[5]

It's no different with parenting. This book is about developing good techniques and correcting bad habits. But more than that, it's about developing a philosophical foundation for interacting with kids. To do this, we have to take the extremely complex, evolving process of child rearing and distill it down to the basics. A huge task, you may think—but one that's possible.

First, a couple of questions need to be answered.

1. What needs to occur for a child to develop into a highly functional adult?
2. What are the processes that need to be imprinted through parenting?

As a developing human being, we all need:

- Support, to exist;
- Models for
- Imitation, since we learn from observing and copying behaviors;
- Limits on our behavior to function as individuals and in society;
- Education and knowledge for success in life; and
- Spirituality, to give meaning to life and provide guiding principles for ourselves and our children.

The first letters of Support, Modeling, Imitation, Limits, Education, and Spirituality spell **S-M-I-L-E-S** a word that will help remember them.

Some of you might think S-M-I-L-E-S is not masculine enough. We could always come up with something like *frowns* or *scowls* if it would make you more comfortable. Let go of the macho image and think about it. Would you rather come out of the game and have the coach smiling and patting you on the back or have him frowning with anger in his eyes?

When you first set eyes on the mother of your children, did you want her to smile at you? I think so. And it's okay for you to smile. Smiles make life enjoyable and fun. Smiles are healing. Researchers tell us that smiling can add eight years to our lives. Smiles allow you to navigate the challenges of parenting.

Learn to laugh at yourself and with those around you. Laughter is fun. It's rewarding. It's about growing a child. It's exciting and should bring a smile to your face daily. Besides, it's easy to remember S-M-I-L-E-S when you're under pressure and need to make an appropriate intervention.

But let's complicate things a little in order to make it interesting. Somehow, we have to apply the support, modeling for imitation, limits, education, and spirituality concepts. So Dr. T will break it down farther.

With each S-M-I-L-E-S concept, you can intervene in three different ways: physically through touch, emotionally through empathy, or intellectually through teaching.

For example, when you show support physically, you might hug your children. You don't necessarily have to say anything; physically being there is what's important. Good coaches do this instinctively. They give players a pat and send them into the game, which is their way of showing physical support.

To support kids emotionally, you might say, "That was really tough, but you did a good job." That lets them know you understand their feelings. Coaches do the same thing when they tell a player to "go in there and get it done; you can do it."

WHERE'S THE PLAYBOOK?

To support children intellectually, you could teach them how changing their approach might solve the problem. You give them tools to use. A coach will explain how a play that didn't succeed could be done differently to work better the next time it's used. This is a teaching or intellectual process that helps players understand how they should change their behavior or approach.

It may be easier to remember the Physical, Emotional, and Teaching moments by using the acronym P-E-T. Certainly, pets bring smiles to our faces. The association of P-E-T with a favorite dog or other animal reminds me that raising a dog is not unlike raising a child. I hope I won't get in trouble with the SPCA for equating dogs with children. Some dog owners may take offense that their little darlings could be compared to unruly, bad-mannered kids.

This book will push you to explore ways to enhance your capability as a husband and father. We will look at ways to help you raise a happy, healthy child, in part by reflecting on the concepts great coaches emphasize to help their players reach their full potential. An important but often neglected part of parenting will be highlighted—having fun. Let's huddle up, get out there, and, as Larry the Cable Guy says, "Git 'er done."

INSTANT REPLAY

- Remember S-M-I-L-E-S—Support, Modeling, Imitation, Limits, Education, and Spirituality
- Remember P-E-T—Physical, Emotional, and Teaching moments with your kids.
- Show support physically with a hug.
- Support children emotionally by letting them know you understand their feelings.
- Support kids intellectually by giving them tools to use to solve problems.
- Work with your spouse in order to accomplish the goals necessary to produce a happy, healthy child.
- Have fun and learn to laugh.

"Anyone can support a team that is winning; it takes no courage. But to stand behind a team, to defend a team when it's down and really needs you, that takes a lot of courage."

—Bart Starr, legendary Green Bay Packers quarterback and Hall of Fame superstar[6]

CHAPTER 2

DADS AND MOMS ARE DIFFERENT
Jumping Out of a Six-Foot Hole

"One of life's most painful moments comes when we must admit that we didn't do our homework, that we are not prepared." —**Merlin Olsen, Pro Football Hall of Famer**[7]

When it comes to parenting, guys can be at an extreme disadvantage. Biology is simply not on our side. Think about it. We are not built to provide even the most basic needs for raising a child. We can't feed an infant on our own without going to the supermarket or milking a cow. Men just don't possess the necessary equipment given to the female of the species. But the biological advantages go beyond breasts to feed and hips to balance a baby on. Women are on hormones, the parental equivalent of performance-enhancing steroids. Not the Barry Bonds type of steroids—something entirely different.

Female brains and bodies are influenced before and after birth by estrogen and other chemicals. Male bodies and brains are different because they are exposed to testosterone (the male hormone) during fetal development and throughout life. That's why we men don't develop hips and breasts that would allow us to bear children and breast-feed them. Because of the effects of testosterone, our brains are generally not programmed to establish an overpowering maternal instinct. Males and females are different from the earliest stages of development with brains and bodies programmed selectively for different functions in life.

It may appear that I am relegating females to a narrow role of childbearing and rearing. Not at all. I am just pointing out that there are physical differences that make it easier for one gender to perform the necessary functions so we can survive as a species. It's not a social pronouncement, just a biological fact.

Women become even more attuned to parenting when they become pregnant. The hormones related to childbearing and rearing go into overdrive. The afterburners get turned on, and we males get left in the dust.

One of the main hormones that make women super-parents is oxytocin. When oxytocin is secreted during labor, it reduces anxiety and promotes a sense of safety and calm. A natural calming agent, it sets the stage for the crucial process of *attachment*—that strong bond between mother and child. If attachment doesn't take place, the child does not do well and, in primitive societies, may die.

The secretion of oxytocin during labor and delivery ensures that just after birth, when a mother is presented with a red-faced, crying, unattractive—no, downright ugly—infant covered in blood and amniotic fluid, whose head has been distorted by the trip through the birth canal, she becomes immediately bonded to the child. Attachment or bonding is further reinforced when oxytocin is secreted during breast-feeding. Every time a woman holds a baby in her arms to feed it, she is becoming more attached to the child.

So, guys, we are behind in the parenting race from the very beginning. We do not go through labor and delivery, nor do we breast-feed. If we took a poll, I'm sure these events would not be high on a man's top-ten list of experiences he wants to have in life. But, by not experiencing them, males may not establish the same level of immediate bonding or attachment to their kids. This delay may affect our responsiveness when it comes to dealing with infants. In general, we just don't have the same feeling for babies that women do.

An example of how men and women typically respond to infants is illustrated in an interview conducted with Sergeant Kimber Smith of the California National Guard on her return from Iraq. Sergeant Smith had a desk job supporting army reconstruction projects while on tour. She came to view her unit as her family.

When showing the interviewer photos she had taken in Iraq, she said, "This is one of an Iraqi baby. That was the first child I was able to hold in probably ten months. Every female in that office just, whew, swooped around this child. The men were just kind of like, cute, whatever, but the women, we were all over that baby. And for a brief moment I felt normal."[8]

The males in this situation did not show the same interest in the baby as the females. They did not respond to the biological clue the same way. The women were demonstrating *aunt behavior*. When women in a room see a baby, they all have to see it, hold it, and mother it.

Aunt behavior is not unique to humans and has been observed in a number of primates, including monkeys, chimpanzees, and gorillas. In these animal societies that require attachment to take place for survival reasons, males are left out of the process. Humans require more time than any other species to develop into self-sufficient adults. The longer it takes to attain the abilities to function as an adult, the more important bonding and attachment become and this job is most often done by the female of the species.

Yes, there is such a thing as male bonding, but that mostly takes place in an entirely different context. Men also secrete oxytocin and other "bonding hormones," but they do so during times of stress—the exact opposite of women, who require peaceful, quiet surroundings for attachment to take place.

The fact that men are more prone to secrete oxytocin during stressful situations makes sense. In hunter-gatherer societies, men needed to work as a team during the hunt. If they were unable to function collectively as a team, the likelihood of being successful was reduced.

A good example of cooperative behavior is seen with the Native Americans hunting buffalo with bows and arrows. Buffalo are huge, dangerous animals, but because of the ability of the men to work as a team, they were highly successful.

This phenomenon of oxytocin secretion during times of stress results in teamwork and "male bonding." It may explain the devotion soldiers have to their units. Many war veterans will relate that they have never felt closer to anyone in their lives than to the men in their units. Even those who have been severely wounded and have had near-death experiences feel like they have let their units down when they're evacuated out of the theater.

The television series *Band of Brothers*, which followed the 101st Airborne Division during World War II from the Normandy invasion through the Battle of the Bulge, illustrated one recurring theme. Soldiers would refuse to leave their buddies on the line and would go AWOL from hospitals to be with them even though they were severely injured.

The same may hold true for men involved in team sports and explain why they get together and discuss in minute detail games played many years earlier (ad nauseam, according to many of their wives).

Men seem to instinctively understand the idea behind take one for the team, we have to work as a team; teamwork above all, and subordinate individuality for the good of the team.

In today's society, there is a blurring of the traditional sex roles. Men most often have to split their loyalties between job and family. Women, because of their strong attachment to children, more often emphasize taking care of the family as the most important aspect of life. When they are part of a team, they, like Sergeant Smith, may begin to think of other members as family.

There are other hormonal differences found when men and women respond to a stressful event. Jiongjiong Wang, PhD and his colleagues, in researching the effects of stress on the body, note that men appear to secrete higher levels of adrenaline and other stress-reactive hormones.[9] This may account for higher levels of cardiovascular disease, aggression, and immune suppression in males. Estrogen appears to dampen the hormonal stress response in females. If you think about it, road rage tends to be primarily a male-dominated "sport." Our blood boils at a much lower temperature than that of our female counterparts. This quickness to anger can have long-term consequences for us physically as well as emotionally. Cool your jets and you might live as long as your spouse!

Dr. Wang and his group were able to demonstrate variations in male and female brains when they were exposed to stressful experiences. The male response to stress is characterized by *fight-or-flight*. Most men either face the stress head-on and go *to combat with the lion* or decide that *discretion is the better part of valor* and turn tail and run.

DADS AND MOMS ARE DIFFERENT

Females by and large have a different response, which has been characterized as *tend-and-befriend*. When stressed, they attempt to nurture offspring and affiliate with the social group. In other words, they take care of their children first and then attempt to find strength in numbers. These responses ensure survival in situations of extreme threat. Men instinctively jump into the fray, and women make sure the children are safe. All of this goes on, and we don't give it a second thought. How marvelous!

Enough about hormones and what is inherently part of being male or female. Let's look at the nurture part of the nature-versus-nurture paradigm. How important is the child's environment in shaping attitudes towards parenting? Think about it. From a very early age, girls are given dolls to dress and stuffed animals to care for. What do guys get? They are given balls of every description or something "masculine" like building blocks, cars, trucks, and things they can manipulate with their hands. They certainly don't get anything to cradle in their arms. If they did play with dolls, they would be teased and ostracized from the group.

For the most part, little girls get socialized, mostly by their moms, to take care of people. From a very early age, girls are asked to help care for younger siblings and probably have a biological predisposition to do so. When women become pregnant, society begins to prepare them for motherhood. They receive attention from all the females in their social group.

Grandparents, especially grandmothers, eagerly anticipate the new grandchild. They shower the mother with presents for the new baby and give lots of emotional support. All of this culminates in the ritual of the baby shower. Men need not apply. Typically, guys are not socialized to "ooh" "ahh" over baby clothes and diaper bags, but the baby shower process is part of the anticipatory bonding for the expectant mother.

Women in prehistoric hunter-gatherer societies worked together in gathering and preparing food to supplement the meat, fish, and other protein hunted by the males. Women engaged in the gathering and food preparation process, which further strengthened the female bonding process. Similarly in more modern societies, shopping is typically a female activity. For a lot of women, shopping is a social event; for most men, it is a chore. Women tend to be trained to focus on relationships; whereas men tend to focus on accomplishment and results.

Typically, young boys are encouraged to be active and to take a more physical approach to the world. Fathers and sons roughhouse and wrestle. Most boys engage in aggressive types of play that get them ready to exert dominance in a social setting. These activities prepare them to go out and face the world, which is less friendly and secure than the family environment.

From very early in life, there is an expectation that the son will become the "man of the house" and a breadwinner. Unfortunately, this expectation at times places undue burdens on the shoulders of very young boys.

When their fathers have to be away from the family for extended periods of time, boys are sometimes told that they need to take care of, protect, and support their mothers. In actuality, young boys have little capacity to do so. A boy is expected to be a macho man even if he is only eight years old. If something goes wrong in the family when Dad is gone, the eight-year-old is responsible, at least in his own mind. Not good!

As boys grow up, they frequently engage in "manly" activities with their dads. They go fishing and hunting; learn how to throw and catch a ball; attend baseball, basketball, and football games; and watch sports on TV. They are often assigned outdoor chores around the house and other masculine activities associated with being a guy.

Are they naturally attracted to babies as their sisters are? Do they learn how to take care of their little brothers or sisters? Do they learn about giving a baby a bottle or feeding it baby food? Do they even learn about changing a diaper? The answer to all of these questions is *most likely not*. Too often this is characterized as "women's work," which robs young men of crucial experiences that would later help them when they become dads.

Boys might participate in helping prepare food, especially if it's barbecuing with Dad, but will most often not enjoy shopping with Mom like their sisters usually do. Clothes are the least important aspect of a boy's life. Clothes are something to get dirty. Unlike girls, who view clothes as prized possessions, boys stay up nights devising ways to wear holes in them, rip them, and generally destroy them. Dads don't mind seeing boys in patched, ragged jeans (in reality they would like a pair just like their sons'), whereas mothers can become upset if their boys have grass stains on their pants or holes in their shirts. Some moms feel they have failed if they don't present a sparkling, well-dressed child to the world.

Now you may be thinking:

- *How can I ever become a good parent? I haven't undergone the same biological or socialization process as females.*
- *I haven't been taught to be a parent, to take care of children, to nurture, feed, and clothe them. What do I do?*
- *How do I deal with this responsibility?*
- *Am I even necessary? Maybe I shouldn't even try.*

Some men have answered these questions and decided to give up their responsibilities to their children, spouses, and families. It's too overwhelming; they're too far behind; it's too uncomfortable; they can't possibly do it. They see child rearing as a job, which they may or may not want. Without training and experience, they feel that they have little possibility of success—it's a prescription for failure. No wonder we have so many single-parent homes.

It's very rare that women abandon their children. They will endure hardships, make sacrifices, and do anything humanly possible to make sure their children are cared for and safe. We see this in nature all of the time. You don't want to get between a female bear and her cubs. Females of other species nurture their offspring and care for them while the males go about procreating with other females.

Women, when they are feeling their worst, will tell me as a psychiatrist that they would not want to go on if it weren't for their children. They say, "I cannot kill myself; I have to be there for my kids." Men don't typically have the same level of attachment to their children as do women, but it doesn't mean they don't have a responsibility. In general, men don't have the tools, don't have the hormones, and don't have the training!

So you're down and in a hole. So what? When you're jumping out of a six-foot hole, a three-foot-high jump is a world record! You don't have to be a woman to be a good parent. Dad's role in parenting is different from Mom's role but no less important to the production of a quality human being. Maybe we can't breast-feed; maybe we don't have the same type of maternal instinct; but we do have the capacity to be a good—no, an excellent—parent.

As proof that you are needed and can make a tremendous difference, here are some of the sobering statistics that confirm the importance of having a father in the home.

- Children from single-parent homes get involved with the juvenile justice system at a much higher level. If there is no dad in the home, the kid, and ultimately the adult, is more likely to spend time in jail. There is the loss of economic production—if you are in jail, you can't work and support a family. Families without dads do not do well economically. The kids are more likely to grow up in poverty.

- The cost to society is astronomical. Most governors would tell you that the prison systems are black holes when it comes to state budgets. We spend anywhere from thirty to sixty thousand dollars a year to keep somebody in jail. It costs billions to apprehend and prosecute criminals. There are losses in the billions for law-abiding citizens whose property is stolen or misappropriated. Many of these criminals may not have gone astray had their families been more stable and structured with a dad in the home.

- Kids from broken or single-parent homes are much more likely to become involved in drug and alcohol abuse. It may be their entry into the criminal justice system, but it most certainly affects their ability to become productive members of society. Drug and alcohol abuse costs the U.S. economy $100,000,000,000 a year—$100 billion with a capital B. Lives are lost because of drunk driving. There are detrimental physical effects of drugs and alcohol on our bodies, increased health-care costs, losses of production because of absenteeism, and ultimately perpetuation of these problems across generations.

- Kids from no-father homes drop out of school more frequently and, even if they stay in school, don't go as far. Dropouts are less likely to get a good job and more likely to live in poverty.

- There is an increased number of out-of-wedlock pregnancies in children from families without dads. (This is the case for both male and female children from one-parent homes.) Someone has to get these girls pregnant, and more often than not, it's a boy from a broken or single-parent household. The girls are more likely to be blamed for the pregnancy, but the responsibility rests equally on the young men. More out-of-wedlock pregnancies beget more single moms and absent dads. It's a predictable cycle. Unfortunately, the cycles are spiraling further and further downward into a pit of poverty, crime, drug and alcohol abuse, and more single-parent families.

After reading the preceding information about females being better prepared than males to be parents, you probably thought you were going to get off the hook, receive a pass, and get a free ride. No one could possibly hold you accountable. As a guy, you have been hormonally deprived and woefully undersocialized. How could anyone expect you to be a success as a parent? Well, just because your body wasn't exposed to the same performance-enhancing, superparent hormones and you didn't play with dolls, feed babies, change diapers, and become socialized to become a parent, that doesn't mean you can't become a successful dad.

You can do it. No excuses. No alibis. Do whatever it takes. *Just do it! Fake it till you make it.* As the coaches say, "Practice, practice, practice, practice, and practice some more." You're important—no, *you're essential*. You can make the difference between success and failure for a child. Your presence and the presence of other men in families can be instrumental in saving our country's way of life. If the family fails, society will continue to disintegrate, and our country will fall apart. That's how important you are as a dad.

No pressure. It's fourth down, no timeouts, only twenty seconds left, and you're on your opponent's forty-yard line. Your two best receivers are out of the game, and you're behind twenty to twenty-four. It's all on your shoulders, but you'll get it done. I know because by the time you finish reading this book you will have all the knowledge necessary to become that "game-winning" dad.

INSTANT REPLAY

- You don't have to be perfect, and you don't have to live up to the same expectations society has for mothers.
- You don't have to clear the same height if you're jumping out of a six-foot hole, because in this case, a three-foot-high jump would still be a world record.
- You do have to be present physically, emotionally, and spiritually for your family, and this goes a long way toward reaching your goal—becoming an unbeatable dad.
- You have to contribute, be there, show support, and demonstrate that you care. Being there and showing support and that you care is the truest expression of love a man can bestow upon his family.
- Love is not exactly a macho guy term. If you missed out on getting hugs and being told you were loved while growing up, it's difficult to demonstrate that affection toward others—to give that hug or to say you care. If you didn't get it, it's hard to give it. It feels strange and uncomfortable. For those of us who have not experienced the verbal and physical expression of love in our families of origin, it may be a difficult task. But saying it and demonstrating it can be among the greatest gifts a husband and father can give his wife and children.
- You can do it because you are reading this book and you are on your way to becoming a "Gold-Medal" Dad.

> *"Confidence comes from being prepared." —**John Wooden, the first person ever enshrined in the Basketball Hall of Fame as both a player and a coach**[10]*

CHAPTER 3

SUPPORT

An Unsupported Child Cannot Survive

*"Coaching is a profession of love. You can't coach people unless you love them." —**Eddie Robinson, Hall of Fame football coach, Grambling University**[11]*

Support is a "critical element" for human existence. It is the most basic component necessary for raising a child. An unsupported or unnurtured child cannot survive. It's as plain as that. Without the support of parents, children are unable to live on their own. They need us to feed them, clothe them, and most important, hold them.

The importance of physical touch was unfortunately confirmed by a cruel experiment devised by a medieval king. He wanted to discover what language children would speak if no one talked to them. In order to do this, he isolated babies from their mothers. He placed them in a bare room, disallowing contact with anyone except to be quickly fed and changed. The king directed that the babies were not to be touched nor interacted with in any other manner.

The result? His experiment failed, because all of the children died. The infants had adequate food and were kept clean, but being in an environment lacking human interaction and contact, they failed to thrive. Lacking human support and touch, the babies could not survive.

There are multiple dictionary definitions of the word *support*, and almost all of them apply when it comes to parenting kids. The first definition of *support* is "to endure bravely or quietly." Parenting is about commitment and sacrifice. It sometimes feels like an endurance race—the unending marathon. We endure hardships so that our children may have better lives. For the most part, we do this bravely and quietly without recognition or accolades.

Mike Krzyzewski of Duke University basketball fame and the coach of the USA gold-medal basketball team, or "Coach K" as he is better known, said it best when talking about his mother: "The person who has inspired me my whole life is my mom, because she taught me commitment. She sacrificed."[12]

Woody Allen once said, "Eighty percent of success is showing up."[13] I would modify this number to 99 percent when it comes to parenting. Given the opportunity, children will develop normally so long as a parent is consistently there for them.

In the late 1930s and early '40s, an "experiment" was conducted with infants who were placed in orphanages. Some of the children were raised by mentally challenged adults. These "handicapped parents" provided excellent, nurturing care for the babies. The young children developed normally and achieved academically because their surrogate, mentally handicapped parents were there for them 100 percent of the time.

Maybe we place too much emphasis on methods of child rearing and too little on the importance of hanging in there to the bitter end. The determination to complete the race—no matter how much it hurts, how long it takes, or how we have to move ourselves over the finish line—is the most important attribute a parent can possess.

Eddie Cantor, an old vaudeville performer, said, "It takes twenty years to become an overnight success." The same can be said of being a parent. You have to hang in there for "twenty years" to have some idea as to whether or not you have been successful. Even then, you should not be worried about giving yourself a grade. Just be thankful that you completed the race and didn't die in the process. You gave it your best and completed the task, and now it's up to your son or daughter to determine his or her measure of success.

SUPPORT

The second definition of *support* is "to promote the interests or cause of." As parents, we automatically become advocates for our children. We want the best for them. We want to give them every opportunity to succeed and to support them in all their endeavors. A fine balance must be established between *doing for our children and allowing them to develop the capacity to accomplish things themselves.*

Very young children require our presence and backing to a much greater degree than do eight- or nine-year-olds. Many times, allowing adolescents to advocate for themselves teaches them to promote their own interests and develop their own causes in life. Sometimes, the best way to support a child is to get out of the way. There is some risk in doing this, but without appropriate risk-taking, there is no gain.

It's the same in sports. Jolene Nagle, Duke University Women's Volleyball coach, has said, "You must be absolutely committed to your athletes. It is important that they know you will fight to get the best of everything for them."[14]

In the book *The Seven Secrets of Successful Coaches*, one college lacrosse player, when talking about his mentor, notes, "He is the most selfless coach I know. He is always looking out for his players and tries to put us first. I don't think I have ever heard him take credit for a win, but I have heard him take blame when we lost. It really isn't about him."[15]

Players and coaches know that the feeling an athlete has about giving 110 percent during a competition has a lot to do with that person's perception of being supported. *The coach yells at me a lot, but I know he's got my back.* The same goes for children. If they feel someone will stand up for them and be their advocate, they can perform at their highest level.

Another meaning of *support* is "to provide with substantiation (corroborate)." It is important that parents validate their children and their accomplishments. Kids develop an internal picture of themselves that is greatly influenced by their environments.

If children are always given negative feedback, they begin to view themselves as failures. "You never do anything right. Look at these grades; you must be stupid." Negative statements pile up and are incorporated into the child's self-image. Marty Schottenheimer, the former San Diego Chargers coach, said, "You have to create an environment where everybody feels good about themselves and what they do."[16]

Former NCAA football and NFL head coach Lou Holtz has said, "Some parents nurture their child's self-image; others provoke their child's self-loathing. Remember, encouragement builds success; discouragement breeds contempt." Coach Holtz goes on to say, "Give them frequent feedback. In order to keep striving, people must see that their efforts are producing results. Good leaders find small victories and celebrate them publicly."[17]

Still another definition of *support* refers to the most basic type of support children need; that is "to pay the costs to maintain; to provide a basis for existence or subsistence of." We do have to feed, clothe, shelter, transport, and educate our kids. It is a substantial economic commitment, which seems at times never-ending. Unfortunately, kids grow rapidly, which means bigger food bills and a new set of clothes every year. Children feel they need their own space, so this can mean a larger house. Transportation problems occur early as they become involved in sports or other after-school activities. Education becomes more important the older the child gets. The financial burden may seem overwhelming when the prospect of paying for a college education is fast approaching.

As parents, we at times emphasize these material goods and services as being the most important support we give our children. It is nice if you have expensive clothes, steak every night for dinner, the best house on the block, the shiniest and fastest car, and admission to the finest university money can buy. As a child and adolescent psychiatrist, I treat children from families who seem to have every material thing. Very often the kids will tell me they would much prefer having their parents be there for them. They want their parents to be available rather than off earning money to pay for the expensive goodies, which parents believe bring happiness and fulfillment.

"To hold up or serve as a foundation or prop" is another definition of *support*. This speaks to the physical component of support that is necessary for appropriate child development. Children need holding—hug a child every day.

SUPPORT

The final definition of *support* that relates to parenting is "to keep from fainting, yielding, or losing courage, to comfort." There are times when children just need to be held no matter what their age.

Lou Holtz, a coach who has led some of the most masculine, even macho, men in the country, makes the statement, "If we came home every night to loved ones who wrap us in their arms and said, 'I love you and appreciate you,' wouldn't this be a better place? There's only one way to establish this ritual in your home. You hug first."[18]

Coach Holtz recounts his experience at Notre Dame when the school hosted the 1987 Special Olympics. Every one of the participants who finished the race had an official hugger. Coach Holtz was in charge of lane three. "No matter who ran in the lane or where they finished—first, last, or anywhere in between—my job was to wrap him or her in a big hug and say, 'I am proud of you, and I love you.'"[19]

> *"Don't wait for a crisis to show someone you care; demonstrate your feelings at every opportunity. We can so enhance our lives if we understand that everyone we meet is asking, 'Do you care about me?' Answer them with some tangible demonstration of your affection."* **—Coach Holtz**[20]

Coach Holtz is not the only prominent leader in athletics who believes showing athletes that you care is an important part of being an effective leader. Tom Osborne, the former University of Nebraska football coach, said, "At Nebraska, our coaching staff was encouraged to genuinely love and care about their players. In other words, each of them was expected to demonstrate an unconditional positive regard towards a player's total well-being." Coach Osborne went on to say, "The traditional coaching style is often that of a drill sergeant who motivates through intimidation and fear. As the years went by, I became more convinced that love was stronger than any source of motivation, even fear."[21]

In order to support our children, we must at times put their well-being ahead of our own. John Wooden, one of the all-time basketball coaching greats, said that one of his pillars of coaching was based on the following statement: "Consider the rights of others before your own feelings, and the feelings of others before your own rights."[22]

All of Coach Wooden's players knew that he put them first and would do everything possible to ensure their success as players and individuals. Another example of putting others first is Coach Woody Hayes. Unfortunately, Coach Hayes is often remembered only for "clothes-lining" an opposition player on the sidelines during a bowl game. Lou Holtz, in his book, recounts that this "short tempered, cantankerous perfectionist had a heart as big as a football field."[23]

"Woody Hayes loved people. He turned down pay raises for himself and said those increases in pay should go to his assistants."[24] According to Coach Holtz, Coach Hayes thought his young assistants needed the money more than he did because they had young families to raise. Lou knew this firsthand because he was one of those young coaches. Coach Hayes understood the need to support not only his players but the rest of his coaching team as well. This is not unlike the family structure, which requires a supportive relationship between the parents in order to succeed.

Well, how can we put this support system into place for our children? And how can you use it on a daily basis in order to become a better dad? Let's look at support from a physical, emotional, and teaching perspective (P-E-T).

Physical Support

How can you be supportive from a physical point of view? That really depends on a number of factors. We've already discussed how men generally are supportive to their families and children. Previously, men were viewed as the breadwinners, the person in the family responsible for bringing in the money. In many families, this is now a shared responsibility in order to make ends meet. But many men still view providing the family with food, clothes, and shelter as fulfilling the commitment to support their children. They understand that taking care of basic survival needs is a key part of support. There's another aspect, however, to physical support. Here we are talking about actually touching and holding children. Women do this instinctively. When a baby cries, they pick it up; when a young child gets hurt, they hold the child and offer consolation; when adolescents are crying and emotionally upset, women give a hug.

SUPPORT

Dads seem to have more difficulty demonstrating physical affection and support. For a guy, it is generally a pat on the back. When kids are crying, men often become uncomfortable. They feel that they have to do something to stop the crying immediately. Men don't recognize that the best way to handle the situation is to be physically present during this time of upset.

Putting an arm around the shoulders, holding a hand, giving a hug, or rubbing an injured arm all provide the physical touch, support, and comfort that will make the tears go away. Words aren't always necessary. Guys feel they have to say something, and often it's the wrong thing. "Don't cry. Be a man. If you stop crying, I'll get you an ice cream cone." being there is enough; the crying will stop on its own.

Men are even less inclined to be physically supportive to their sons. It's okay to roughhouse with them but not to pick them up and hold them when they've hurt themselves. It's a macho thing. We think we have to teach them to be tough. In reality, however, this makes things more difficult for the kids in the long run. They don't develop a comfort level with physical closeness, which has long-lasting ramifications for their relationships with future wives and children.

Guys find it easier to comfort their young daughters. It's easier to accept a hug from their special little girls than to go out of the way to hug their young sons. However, there is a very awkward time for fathers and daughters related to the onset of adolescence, which comes with the development of curves in their little babies. Dad is confronted with another "woman" in the family, and this may be so uncomfortable as to disturb his relationship with his daughter. The young woman may view this distancing as rejection and may then seek affection from a male outside the family.

As a child and adolescent psychiatrist, I often have heard from female adolescent patients who became involved early in premarital sexual relationships that they really did not enjoy sex. They only wanted to be physically held, and sex was just the price they had to pay to be held. So, dads, hug your daughters and your sons.

As Coach Holtz said, "Don't hide your love. Everyone needs a hugger."[25] When you're interacting with your child and you don't know what to do, you can never fail if you give a hug, a touch, or a pat on the back.

Emotional Support

What does emotion really mean anyway? This is a tough one for men because we're not supposed to be emotional. We are trained throughout our lives to be stoic and emotionless. It's okay to get mad, but you can't feel sad and show it. We hear, "Little boys don't cry. You're just a sissy when you cry. Take it like a man." Responding in these ways makes it hard to identify our own emotions, much less the emotions of others.

Women have much more experience in recognizing and responding to how other people feel. They understand how someone might feel when a loved one is lost, and they can demonstrate emotional support by recognizing the sadness of the loss and by expressing their concern. If the person with the loss cries and shows emotion, a woman feels reinforced. She helps the individual work through a tough time and knows it was important for him or her to shed tears over the loss.

A guy in the same situation might say nothing at all, and if the person did shed tears, the guy would feel very uncomfortable. He would think, *Boy, I screwed up. I should not have mentioned it; I just made them cry. Now what do I do?*

Guys, let me tell you, being supportive emotionally is really not that tough. It may seem awkward at first, but stating the obvious is an excellent way of demonstrating emotional support.

- If your son or daughter comes crying in the door after wrecking his or her bike, your response might be, "Boy, I bet that hurt a lot. Let's do something to fix it up."

You just demonstrated that you understand that he or she is hurting and that you're going to help him or her deal with it.

- When your child's team loses a game, you might say, "Losing that one was really tough. I'd be upset, too. But you did your best, and that's what counts."

You're supportive emotionally in several different ways during that interaction. You're teaching that losing is the pits, but it's part of reality; you can't win them all. You're telling your child that he or she is not a bad person and

SUPPORT

it's okay to be upset about losing, but he or she has to put it in perspective and move on.

Your child learns that doing his or her best in any situation is more important than winning or losing. You're being extremely supportive, identifying your child's emotions and making a positive out of a negative. Letting your child know you understand the emotions he or she is experiencing helps the child feel supported and loved.

There may be times, especially when dealing with teenagers, that your attempts to be emotionally supportive will be rejected. This is part of their being adolescents and establishing independent identities.

- Your son or daughter may come home from school complaining about the unfairness of a specific teacher. "That test was unfair. She never helps me, and I hate that class." In your most supportive voice, you might say, "Sounds like you're pretty mad." Your favorite teenager might respond sarcastically, "Yeah, duh, Dad. Are you some kind of therapist now?"

You might feel like saying, "No, you little so-and-so, but I will 'therapize' your behind if you keep that up." But you don't have to carry it any further. You've said your piece; it did register, and although you didn't get the response you wanted, it was secretly appreciated. You'll know you succeeded when he or she continues to vent about the unfairness of the whole educational system. Welcome to the teenage years. They are trying times but fun if you keep your sense of humor and perspective.

It's hard to deal with the less pleasant emotions such as anger, sadness, fear, anxiety, and disappointment when we talk about emotional support. Those are emotions that may be more difficult for men to recognize and especially verbalize. It's not really that tough, however.

Here are some examples of what you might say.

- Boy, you sound angry. What's going on?
- Hey, you look sad; tell me about it.

- I was really scared the first time I jumped off the high dive, but I got over it.

- You know, it's normal to be anxious before the game. Heck, some professional athletes throw up before they go on the field.

- It's really disappointing when you don't get the grade you're expecting. But if you work hard, I'm sure you'll do better next time.

The best way you can support children emotionally is to give them encouragement, an emotional boost, whenever they do something positive. When your baby toddles across the room to you for the first time, you can say, "Good job!" You may think that your baby's too young to understand, but he or she will pick up on the tone of your voice and the smile on your face, and associate those with the words. Besides, if you start saying "good job" for all the positive behaviors of your toddler, you will be training yourself to be a positive-thinking dad. It doesn't always have to be "good job." You can say, "That's great! Wow, look at you go! Fantastic! Splendiferous! Outstanding! Wonderful!" Develop a list of positive words and use them as frequently as possible. Be enthusiastic in your praise and do it often.

There is an old saying: When working with people of all ages, give ten positive statements to one criticism.

If you are emotionally supportive ten out of eleven times that you interact with your child, he or she will respond better to the one time that you have to be critical. Lots of positives help children feel good about themselves, develop positive self-esteem, and be able to accept criticism.

But let's be even more positive and shoot for ninety-nine supportive interactions to one critical one. Get started right now! Make that list of positive, supportive words and phrases and use one of them the next time you see your child. You can read all about it and say it's a good idea, but you have to put it into action. Do it now! I'm positive you'll succeed.

In order to be emotionally supportive, just state the obvious, and you'll be surprised by the results. Put yourself in the same situation and think about how you might feel. It hurts when you hit your thumb with a hammer. You feel upset and angry when you don't get the job promotion you were counting on. You're sad if you lose a close friend.

Your kids will experience the same feelings you do, but in a different developmental framework. They may fall down and hurt themselves, not win the game they were playing with their friends, or have a best friend move out of town. You can identify the feelings associated with those experiences for your children. By doing this, you then allow them to express their emotions in an appropriate manner, and you have taught them an invaluable life lesson. Good job; keep it up. You're a "gold-medal" dad.

Teaching Support

How can I teach support? The answer is you have already been doing it. The way you raise your children will directly influence the way they raise your grandchildren.

- You are teaching by example when you are positive, supportive, and enthusiastic.
- You support them intellectually by teaching them how to conquer the challenges of life. This takes place incrementally as they grow and develop. With a preschooler, you may explain the rules of Chutes and Ladders. Your young son may want to learn about cars, fishing, basketball, or chess. Your daughter may be involved in basketball, soccer, computers, or debate. They have to learn the concept behind the games before they can participate and enjoy the activity.
- You explain things, sometimes over and over, so your children can understand and succeed. You may learn a few things yourself, but it is your interest and participation in the process that counts.

Dads support their children intellectually by giving them learning experiences that will expand their horizons. They encourage reading and other intellectual pursuits. As a supportive father, you assist them when they're having difficulties academically and praise them for even the smallest accomplishment. Completing a difficult math problem, finishing a science project, writing a poem, or drawing a picture are small victories in the quest for academic success.

INSTANT REPLAY

- To support our children, we must at times put their well-being ahead of our own.
- Don't hide your love. Give your child a hug or a pat on the back.
- State the obvious to show you understand as a way of demonstrating emotional support.
- Give kids encouragement.
- Become a positive-thinking dad.
- Keep your sense of humor and perspective.

*"You must have respect, which is part of love, for those under your supervision. Then they will do what you want and more."—**John Wooden, voted "Coach of the Century" by ESPN*** [26]

SECOND QUARTER

Cleaning your house while your kids are still growing up is like shoveling the walk before it stops snowing. —**Phyllis Diller**

"Fatherhood is pretending the present you love most is soap on a rope." —**Bill Cosby**

"I believe that we parents must encourage our children to become educated so they can get into a good college that we cannot afford." —**Dave Barry, newspaper columnist**

CHAPTER 4

MODELING FOR IMITATION
Monkey See; Monkey Do

"Young people need models, not critics." —***John Wooden***[27]

Modeling is the most underrated aspect of learning. We learn more by observation and copying the behavior of others than by any other method. "A picture is worth a thousand words" is the old saying. We only have to look at nature to understand the importance of modeling behaviors. This is especially true for carnivores. Mother bears, lions, wolves, foxes, and even house cats teach their offspring how to hunt. This requires time, so most juvenile carnivores need constant attention after they're born and stay with their mothers for at least two years. They need time to learn the intricacies of tracking, pursuing, and ambushing prey. It is interesting to note that prey animals like deer, elk, rabbits, and wild sheep leave their mothers earlier than other animals. You don't need much training to run away.

When we look at primates such as chimpanzees, orangutans, and the great apes, we see many behaviors that they model for their youngsters. You might remember Jane Goodall's documentation of chimpanzees using tools. A mother chimpanzee would break off a twig or sturdy piece of grass, wet it with her lips, and stick it into a termite mound to extract a mid-afternoon snack. Her offspring would dutifully observe her behavior and then imitate it themselves. Goodall validated the saying "monkey see; monkey do."

Human infants begin modeling behaviors early in their development. They learn to make eye contact almost immediately. A mother will coo and talk "baby talk" to her infant, and the child responds by imitation. Children will come to understand and speak the language used by their mothers and other members of the family. They will speak it with the same accent, inflections, and vocabulary as their parents.

When we teach children how to throw a ball, we don't give them a set of incomprehensible instructions translated to English from Chinese (like we get in that toy set we have to assemble on Christmas Eve). And we don't try to explain it verbally. Can you imagine going through the following scenario?

> *First, you grasp the ball in your hand; raise it next to your ear with your palm facing forward; your elbow should be pointing outwards; the wrist is cocked backwards, and as the arm moves forward, the wrist is un-cocked, and the ball is released.*

No, we pick up the ball and throw it to them. They watch, catch the ball, and throw it back. We may make minor adjustments to their technique, but they learn by imitating.

We now know that human brains are programmed to imitate behavior from infancy. If you stick your tongue out at a newborn, it will reciprocate. Humans have a sophisticated network of mirror neurons in our brains, which allow us to imitate the actions of others in our environment. These brain cells are activated during the learning process and even make it possible to anticipate the behavior of those around us. Children's brains are hardwired to imitate and incorporate everything in their environment as part of normal development. Now, that is scary.

Every day, children watch our behaviors and actions—no, they scrutinize them. Whatever we do is observed and recorded in their little brains for use in the future. They imitate our gestures, our expressions, and our physical demeanors. Look at Johnnie; he's got the same walk as his dad. Susie loves playing dress-up in her mother's old clothes. How cute! She put on her mother's makeup, and she's only three. Children are programmed to model the behaviors and attitudes of the adults in their lives. For this reason, parents need to ask themselves, "What were my role models like?" and "What kind of a role model do I want to be?"

MODELING FOR IMITATION

When it comes to parenting, Yogi Berra said it best: "It's like déjà vu all over again." Yogi was right. We parent like we were parented. Our role models, however imperfect, have had a significant impact on our parenting styles and abilities. Some of our parents may not have been the best role models, so Yogi's statement, "If you can't imitate him, don't copy him," may hold true. There are times when we don't want to model ourselves after our parents and imitate their parenting styles.

"Our chief want is someone who will inspire us to be what we know we could be." **—Ralph Waldo Emerson**[28]

As a child psychiatrist stationed with the United States Army in Germany in the late 1970s, I was talking with a sergeant who was having problems with one of his young children. We were discussing discipline and how his attitude had changed over the years. He said, "Before, I would spank my kids pretty hard, but now I only give a swat on the butt with my bare hand. My dad spanked me regularly with a fairly thick belt. His dad used a heavy-weight razor strap on him, and my great-grandfather beat my granddad with a bullwhip."

Through the generations, methods of discipline were modified but not without considerable difficulty. Our sergeant decided he didn't need to use a belt, but his father told him that he was being too easy on his kids. He knew he was doing the right thing because he confided in me that physical punishment didn't work very well anyway. But he was looked down on by the rest of the family because of his "lenient" approach to parenting.

Unfortunately, as said by Oliver Goldsmith, "People seldom improve when they have no model but themselves to copy."[29]

At times, as parents, we have to look outside ourselves for the answer to our parenting dilemmas. Like the sergeant who was having second thoughts about his parenting style, we may require other role models to imitate. We may need to alter those ingrained patterns of behavior that were modeled after our parents and relatives. This requires hard work and research. We must observe those around us and see how they carry themselves.

Advice from successful coaches:

> *"It isn't what you do, but how you do it."* —**John Wooden, one of the winningest coaches in basketball history**[30]

> *"We learn by watching people complete a task, not by looking at the finished product."* —**Dr. T**

> *"You can observe a lot by just watching."* —**Yogi Berra**[31]

> *"Choose your role models carefully and only after prolonged observation."* —**Dr. T**

Actions speak louder than words, so it's important to watch what you do as well as what you say as a parent. You never know when one of your little "treasures" will be watching. One of them will always be present when you use language you shouldn't be using or behave in a way that reflects poorly on you and your family. You can count on it. The @#*&% you let slip out when you banged your thumb will be blurted by your son or daughter at a party for your boss or, more likely, in church.

> *"Get to know yourself: you can't improve upon something you don't understand. The more questions you ask yourself, the better you'll know yourself."* —**Vince Lombardi, the great Green Bay Packers coach**[32]

If you're going to be a role model, you have to look in the mirror. You have to scrutinize your behavior and assess the impact it may have on an impressionable child. Coach Lombardi further states, "To be successful, you've got to be honest with yourself. Improvements in moral character are our responsibility. Bad habits are eliminated, not by others but by ourselves. If you're going to ask people to respect your authority, you need to lead by example."[33]

The importance of character cannot be overemphasized. We need to model the behaviors we want our children to imitate. We have to build character in ourselves if we want our children to have character. Coach John Wooden emphasized building character in his players so they might succeed in life as well as on the basketball court. He said, "Be more concerned with your character than your reputation, because your character is what you really are, while your reputation is merely what others think you are."[34] General H. Norman Schwarzkopf, "Stormin' Norman" as he was called after his superb performance during the first Gulf War, said, "Leadership is a potent combination of strategy and character. But if you must be without one, be without strategy."[35]

In his book, *The Lombardi Rules*, Vince Lombardi's son quotes his dad as saying, "Building character takes discipline. Internalizing the principles and values you believe in means that they will surface in times of crisis. This takes daily renewal and practice."[36] This is especially valuable advice when applied to parenting. We have to discipline ourselves as parents to uphold certain principles in life and practice these on a daily basis so that they become second nature.

When times get tough, we want to respond instinctively in a way that would make our children and ourselves proud. If you want to be able to respond appropriately under pressure, you need repetition, repetition, repetition, and more repetition. The quarterback couldn't throw the ball to the receiver before he made his cut to the sideline without practicing the route with him over and over again.

We must ask ourselves on a daily basis, "Is this behavior going to demonstrate strength of character to my child?" By repeatedly questioning our actions, we become more aware and, as a result, better role models for our children.

Coach Holtz, in his book *Winning Every Day: The Game Plan for Success*,[37] recounts how his early lack of introspection and self-examination caused difficulties for him and his family. Credit should be given to Coach Holtz for disclosing his own failings because he serves as a positive role model to others. We all make mistakes, but it is the strong among us who can admit their mistakes and learn from them. We become even stronger if, like Coach Holtz, we share those experiences with others.

Coach Holtz talked about the way he would criticize his wife because he was concerned that she might leave him. He stated that his behavior was inexcusable and embarrassing and that it was hard to put down on paper. He said, "I cannot apologize enough for the grief I caused that fine woman." Coach Holtz went on to say he was "once one of the most insecure men you could ever meet. I maligned others, hoping I would look better by comparison. I was degrading myself and bringing misery to those around me."[38]

Other coaches emphasize the need for self-examination. Rick Pitino, University of Louisville men's basketball coach, says, "Leaders need introspection. Knowing yourself, your strengths, your weaknesses, and your values is essential."[39] Coach Holtz further emphasizes the need for introspection, "Never take your attitude for granted. Reevaluate yourself continually to ensure you are maintaining your edge."[40]

Many other sports notables also looked at the importance of self-evaluation. Willie Shakespeare, the outstanding second baseman for the Toledo Mud Hens, said, "This above all, to thine own self be true." The tennis great Virginia Woolf reflected, "If you do not tell the truth about yourself, you cannot tell it about other people." Eric Hoffer, coach of the Detroit No Wings, emphasized, "We lie loudest, when we lie to ourselves." (Okay, so the last three weren't really big sports figures. But you know in their hearts they were wannabes. And besides, what they said was pretty right on.)

> *"There is no pillow as soft as a clear conscience."*
> **—John Wooden**[41]

Modeling Honesty

Honesty is certainly an attribute we want to model for our children. Numerous coaches emphasize honesty as the basis for positive and enduring relationships. Marty Schottenheimer, former coach of the San Diego Chargers, recounts in *The Seven Secrets of Successful Coaches*, "The single most important obligation you have to your athletes is to be honest with them. They are not always going to agree with your decision or think it is fair, but it is your obligation to be honest with them."[42]

In the same book, Coach Mike Krzyzewski emphasizes, "I want our team to know that when I tell them something, it's the truth. They have to know that my word is good. I don't know if there is a bigger issue for me. In the long run, I believe most people respect and appreciate someone who is honest with them."[43]

Our children expect—no, demand—honesty from us at all times. If we are dishonest, we lose trust. If we lose trust, we lose a relationship. Modeling honesty all the time is tough. We can't fudge on our taxes or cheat in Chutes and Ladders and expect our children to be trustworthy, honest adults. Of course, there are other benefits to being honest. If you've been honest with yourself and others during the day, you will sleep very well that night. No self-doubt, no guilt will keep you awake.

Will Rogers, the homespun humorist of the mid twentieth century, quipped, "Live so that you wouldn't be ashamed to sell the family parrot to the town gossip." Being honest and forthright both at home and in public takes much of the worry out of life. A truthful person can be trusted and will gain respect from family and friends.

When asked about how you can obtain the trust of others, Lou Holtz responded, "The answer is surprisingly simple: Just do right. Live an honorable life. Do what is right and avoid what is wrong."[44] Not bad advice if you want to be a good role model for your kids.

Modeling Appropriate Physical Behavior

When we consider being a role model for our children to imitate, we need to consider how we physically model appropriate behavior. This may mean teaching our kids by taking care of our bodies in a way that promotes health and physical safety.

We can't expect our children to refrain from reckless and risky behaviors if we engage in them ourselves.

- "Johnnie, don't stand too close to the edge!" Meanwhile, Dad is leaning out trying to get that unusual camera angle and is reprimanded by the park ranger for his behavior.
- Dad lectures his children on the importance of off-road safety but conveniently leaves his helmet off when he climbs on the four-wheeler.

The most important part of this physical aspect of modeling relates to personal fitness. There's Dad sitting in his favorite lounge chair drinking a beer, smoking a cigarette, and going on about the *lack of physical fitness programs in our schools*. The rest of the family is munching on chips and dip while busily writing down a recipe for chocolate cake with cream cheese icing being shown on the Food channel.

How can we expect to produce healthy and fit children if we don't take care of ourselves? Do we want to doom our kids to a lifelong struggle with obesity, diabetes, and heart disease? This issue is so crucial to the well-being of our children that I have devoted two chapters later in the book to diet and exercise. Fit and trim parents turn out fit and trim offspring.

Modeling Emotional Behavior

Emotions! Emotions! Emotions!—words that strike terror in the hearts of men. It's tough enough trying to manage our own emotions. How can we help our kids?

Men are better at expressing anger but sometimes can't even get that right. They think raising their voices and getting in someone's face equates with being manly and macho. Lawrence Peter said, "Speak when you are angry, and you'll make the best speech you ever regret." Most of the time, the quiet approach is much more appropriate and productive.

If something makes you mad, say so immediately. Don't hold it in, let things build up, and then come out with a long string of expletives. You just have to say, "That makes me angry, please stop." say what you feel, when you feel it. Don't wait until you explode. That doesn't sound so hard, does it? You just have to think about it and *practice it*.

Now comes the tough part: dealing with sadness. Guys just seem to be put off by tears. They typically can't handle someone else's crying, much less show that kind of emotion themselves. It's as if shedding tears would drain them of their manhood, leaving them weak and vulnerable. It's acceptable for men to cry after they win a state championship but not if they have lost a close friend.

Sadness is part of life. When dads model how to genuinely express sadness, they give a great gift to their children, especially to their sons. You often hear, "only sissies cry" "be a man." Telling children not to express emotions appropriate to the situation limits their capacity to function in future relationships. Boys are more likely to have later difficulties with emotions than girls because guys have a more limited range of expression. It's just like the boy who played with the truck while his sister fed and nurtured her doll—young boys didn't learn how to take care of infants and certainly did not learn that it's okay to cry.

> *"The most essential thing for a leader to have is the respect of those under his or her supervision. It starts with giving them respect."* **—John Wooden**[45]

> *"My ideas about how to command respect have changed. I have learned that you can't demand it or whack it out of people with a two by four. You have to cultivate it in yourself and those around you."*—**Pat Summitt, coach of the University of Tennessee's women basketball team and one of the most successful coaches of all time**[46]

Modeling Respect

Respect is a quality that all parents want their children to learn and practice. Two great basketball coaches with very similar philosophies, Pat Summit and John Wooden, understand the need for people in authority to respect those they hope to influence. It's the same with parenting. We will not have the respect of our children unless we model it for them and respect them as well.

There is a very easy way to make sure that respect is an integral part of family interactions. I learned a very important lesson on respect from a rugby teammate who managed a restaurant. I complimented him on his service staff and asked how he was able to keep his workers happy. I knew that turnover was especially high for workers in this business. He said, "Two words, *please* and *thank you*." All employees were required to say "please" if they made a request and "thank you" if they received anything at all. This meant that the servers, the busboys, the chefs, the dishwashers, and he himself were all held accountable for demonstrating respect toward others. If he slipped and forgot to say "please" or "thank you," he was fined a specific amount, which would go toward an employee party at the end of the year.

When we talk about respect, it has to start at the top. Mom and Dad need to demonstrate respect toward each other if they expect their children to follow suit. The please-and-thank-you rule needs to go into effect immediately. If a child learns to say "please" and "thank you" from a very early age, he or she has a head start on developing positive relationships in life. Because of daily repetition, respectful interactions become second nature. They are instinctive and will come to the fore under pressure.

INSTANT REPLAY

- To be a role model, you have to look in the mirror.
- Lead by example.
- Build character by upholding certain principles in life and practicing them on a daily basis.
- Honesty is the basis for positive and enduring relationships.
- Take care of your body in a way that promotes health and safety.
- Express emotions appropriately, and don't hold your feelings inside.
- Respect yourself and your children will respect you.
- Please and thank you, please and thank you, please and thank you.

"Players don't care how much I know until they know how much I care." —**Frosty Westerling,** *whose overall record in forty-eight seasons as a college coach is 305–96–7, who won four national championships, and who is the owner of the tenth-most wins in NCAA history.* [47] *Which college was lucky enough to have him on board?*

CHAPTER 5

LIMITS

You Gotta Live Within Them, Can't Live Without Them

"The really free person in society is the one who is disciplined. Players feel loved when they are disciplined." —Dean Smith, UNC basketball coach for thirty-nine years[48]

The concept of limits is very difficult for many to understand. Limits mean different things to different people. Nobody likes to be told no. We all are concerned about the limits placed on us by society and especially the government. We're told every day what we can and cannot do, and very often we resent this intrusion on our freedom.

As adults, we complain about necessary limits on our behavior and freedoms. All too often, we express these inappropriate opinions in front of our children. We then expect them to obey authority without question. It is okay for us to exceed the speed limit so long as it "doesn't hurt anybody." "Officer, I was only ten miles an hour over the speed limit. Can't you overlook it this time?" And so it goes. "It was just one fish over the limit. I can't believe you're giving me a fine!" You complain, "Why do we have to pay taxes anyway? The government is just going to waste the money." You think the cop in the patrol car is out to get you. "Why can't the police go after the real criminals—the ones that are robbing banks and committing murders? No, they have to lie in wait to catch someone driving too fast in a school zone. Twenty-five miles an hour is way too slow, and it always makes me late to work."

Vince Lombardi's pronouncement should serve as a guide for all parents: "You gotta remember one thing. If you're going to exercise authority, you've got to respect it."[49] So listen to Coach Lombardi and understand that your moaning and groaning is teaching your children to grow up to be complainers and whiners. Remember, you are a role model.

As parents, we have the responsibility of setting limits for our children. This part of the developmental process is necessary for them to develop the capacity to set limits for themselves. When we have difficulty setting limits for ourselves, we make it doubly difficult for our children to learn. They will have negative role models, and they will also lack the experience of developing their own limit-setting abilities.

If we observe nature, we see how animals set limits for their offspring. If a kitten strays from its mother, it is gently retrieved and placed back in the box. When a puppy is play-fighting and bites too hard, it will receive a nip from its parent. When kittens are able to forage on their own, the mother cat no longer allows them to suckle. Baby birds are no longer fed and are summarily booted out of the nest when they are able to fly. This weaning process takes place in many animal species and constitutes an important limit-setting milestone for the mother and her offspring.

Humans are no different. They are weaned from their mothers' breast milk and transitioned to solid foods. Ten-year-olds are not allowed to breast-feed for obvious reasons. Ultimately, our children need to grow up and leave the nest. Some children impose themselves on their parents well into adulthood because their parents have difficulty setting limits. This situation leads to unhealthy relationships and interrupts a normal developmental process. The children who have not been allowed to become independent are doomed to failure emotionally and financially because of this lack of separation. Of course, if you don't have to do anything for yourself and no one is going to hold you accountable, why should you leave?

> *"Human beings are the only creatures on earth that allow their children to come home."*
> *—**Bill Cosby**[50]*

We often equate limit-setting with discipline. A strict parent is characterized as being a strong disciplinarian. Someone who sets very firm limits and maintains them in the face of criticism is often scorned by those who have problems setting limits. Disciplining others is always tough, but it is an essential part of parenting. When considering discipline, we must look to ourselves first. Self-discipline should come first at all times. We cannot expect our children to respond to our limit-setting if we don't set limits for ourselves. Someone once said that the best leaders are those who know how to follow. You have to set the example. You have to set limits for yourself in order to set limits for others.

Coaches understand the need for discipline and commitment. If you are to set limits for others, you can't be concerned about what others think. Lou Holtz, when talking about his good friend Woody Hayes, related that Coach Hayes would never compromise his standards to win friends. "Woody, in fact, didn't care if anybody liked him. Woody was completely himself, which is probably why he earned the admiration of everyone he touched."[51] As a parent, you can't be concerned about what the neighbors or even the grandparents think about the discipline you mete out to your children.

There is a fine line between being a harsh disciplinarian and appropriately setting limits. As Coach Holtz related in his book, "We can never minimize the importance of discipline mixed with love. When you genuinely love someone, discipline is the tool to spur them to greater heights. However, there is a thin line between discipline and harassment." Coach Holtz elaborates on establishing consequences for negative behaviors. He would ask himself the question "Will this punishment make this individual a better person, athlete or student?" He added, "If your answer is yes, then you are administering discipline. If the answer is no, then it is harassment. Avoid it at all costs."[52]

John Wooden had similar thoughts about being a coach: "I didn't want to be a dictator to my players or assistant coaches or managers. For me, concern, compassion, and consideration were always priorities of the highest order."[53]

Criticism can be viewed as a part of discipline, but criticism without compassion rarely has a positive effect. Coach Holtz said, "When you're loaded with criticism, don't pull the trigger." Coach Wooden defined it best: "A coach is someone who can give correction without causing resentment."[54]

Unfortunately, many models we have for setting limits and correcting behaviors are those coaches on the sidelines yelling at players who've made mistakes. Although there are successful coaches who are impassioned and highly vocal when expressing their displeasure with an athlete's less-than-perfect performance, they are generally the exception rather than the rule.

The successful coach who yells and demonstrates his or her frustration usually has developed a positive and caring relationship with the team members. The players will perform because they know the coach truly cares about them, and they understand that the apparent anger is not directed at them personally.

Children are no different. They can accept negative traits in their parents as long as they feel cared for and respected. Yelling and screaming are not effective methods of achieving compliance and improving performance in the long run. When you become frustrated and angry, you lose your effectiveness as a parent. Explosions of emotion, especially anger, generate fear but rarely correct the problem. Coach Wooden said, "Pride is a better motivator than fear. Remember, pride comes when you give respect."[55] It's hard for a child to have a feeling of respect if all he or she hears is criticism, criticism, criticism. To quote Coach Holtz, "Like the old song says, you have to accentuate the positive, but don't hype it. As long as you keep your criticism constructive, you can help people build on their assets by pointing out their liabilities."[56]

Setting limits is synonymous with setting standards. Vince Lombardi believed that the quality of a person's life is in direct proportion to his or her commitment to excellence, regardless of his or her chosen endeavor.[57] We have to establish goals in our lives and show self-discipline to work toward those goals every day of our lives. In order to overcome adversity, we must set limits for ourselves and demonstrate to our children the meaning of accomplishment. Coach Holtz goes on to say, "If life is a classroom, adversity is its teacher. We can't lower our standards during hard times. We must raise them."[58] Coach Lombardi related, "Leaders are made, they are not born. They are made by hard effort, which is the price which all of us must pay to achieve any goal that is worthwhile."[59]

Self-discipline, goal-setting, and working hard to achieve goals are attributes parents can model for their children every day. "If things came easy, then everybody would be great at what they did, let's face it."[60] This is Coach "Iron" Mike Ditka's statement about the need to work hard to achieve success. He goes on to say, "If you are determined enough and willing to pay the price, you can get it done."[61] Lou Holtz relates, "If you settle for nothing less than your best, you'll be amazed at what you can accomplish in life."[62] To further emphasize the point, Coach Holtz exclaims, "No one has ever drowned in sweat!"[63]

We have to work hard at being parents. It's a full-time job with daily challenges that will tax our physical, emotional, and intellectual capacities. But parenting is made easier by breaking down our daily tasks into small achievable goals. We often become overwhelmed when we think about the big picture, the future, and all those negative things over which we have no control.

Mark Twain once said, "Make it a point to do something every day that you don't want to do."[64] If you can do this on a daily basis, you will establish a pattern of behavior that will allow you to achieve in all areas of your life. By modeling this type of self-discipline for your children, you will impart to them the capacity to succeed in each and every endeavor in their lives.

Like Coach Holtz emphasizes, "You can't accomplish anything big without doing the little things."[65] It always goes back to the fundamentals and the willpower to practice these success-building behaviors over and over and over. *Practice, practice, practice.*

Physical Limits

When setting limits for children, it is essential to consider their developmental level. Some of this will seem self-evident and quite simple, but going over the basics is essential to success in the long run. As with support and modeling, we will break down limit-setting into physical, emotional, and teaching components (P-E-T). These will naturally overlap to a degree, but keeping them in mind will make it easier to determine the best approach in various real-life situations.

The physical aspect of limit-setting is more likely to be used with younger children. If your two-year-old is about to run into traffic, you instinctively grab him or her to prevent a catastrophe from happening. You pick up the child whose hand is about to touch a hot burner on the stove and tell him or her "no." A problem arises with limits when the child is not in extreme danger. At these times, frequently parents are reluctant to intervene physically. They may be busy or trying to relax when their toddler is going after a family heirloom or some other highly breakable item.

As a child psychiatrist, I see parents of very young children attempting to set limits verbally rather than intervening physically to stop inappropriate or dangerous behavior.

- They will say from across the room, "Sammy, don't climb on the table." Sammy glances over his shoulder and with a look of determination continues to climb with his gaze fixed on the irreplaceable vase bequeathed to the family by Great-Grandma.
- Another call from across the room: "Sammy, get down from there this instant." The voice is slightly raised but not yet a shout. By this time, Sammy is close to the prized possession, eagerly reaching out his little hand while glancing back to see if his increasingly frustrated parent is going to act. Sure enough, he finally reaches his destination and, while attempting to pick up the much-admired prize, knocks it off the table. It crashes loudly to the floor.
- At this point, Dad is enraged and leaps out of the recliner, spilling his drink and yelling at the top of his lungs that he will teach this unruly three-year-old a thing or two.

TIME-OUT!

How could this play have been executed better?

What do we need to practice?

When setting limits for young children, it is important to follow verbal commands quickly with physical intervention if the desired response does not occur immediately.

LIMITS

I know it's a pain to get up out of your chair and set the physical limit, but that is an essential technique in training your child to respond to one verbal command. If you do not intervene quickly but continue over and over with halfhearted requests to stop, you are teaching your child to ignore your verbal commands until you finally become angry enough to intervene physically. This often results in giving corporal punishment.

As children get older, they generally require fewer physical limit-setting interventions. They do, however, need other physical experiences with their fathers.

- Rough-and-tumble play is something fathers engage in with their children naturally. Although it may be uncomfortable for dads to cradle an infant in their arms, they have no difficulty tossing the baby into the air, much to the chagrin of the horrified mom.
- Guys have a basic need to interact physically with their children. Rolling around on the floor and giving them rides on their backs or shoulders seem to come naturally. This type of physical contact is extremely important for normal development.

We are only now becoming aware of the significance of these physical interactions between fathers and their children. The rough-and-tumble play appears to affect the development of personal physical boundaries and helps children deal more appropriately with anger. Children who have experienced this type of physical contact are much less likely to be violent as they get older. They learn through the play-fighting how to place limits on their own aggressive behavior.

This is not unlike young puppies roughhousing with older dogs as a way of learning how to limit their aggressiveness. If they bite too hard, they receive a nip in return. This immediately teaches them the need to place limits on their aggressive behavior.

When we think of roughhousing, we often envision a dad and his sons wrestling in the living room. We now know that it is extremely important for young girls to be involved in this type of physical play, too. They need the same type of physical interaction to develop their own sense of physical competence and mastery of their aggressive feelings. They feel more confident and are more willing to stand up for themselves in potentially violent situations. They may be less likely to tolerate abusive relationships and demonstrate more assertiveness in their interactions with men.

So, guys, wrestle with your kids. It's fun! When they get to have physical contact with their dad, you're helping them become more self-confident and assertive.

Emotion and Limits

All too often, parents do not place enough emotion in their voices so that children know they mean business the first time a request is made or a command is given. What I mean by emotion is an increase in volume and a deepening in pitch. When you say no, you should say it emphatically. *NO!* You do not need to yell, but display firmness in your tone and an expression on your face that indicates you mean business. It's like that frown you saw from the coach when you took that ill-advised shot in basketball, missed the tackle in football, or ignored a sign in baseball. Kids pick up on our emotions, and we should use them to communicate.

If you're going to tell a child no, do it with some feeling and enthusiasm. This is one area where men seem to have an advantage over females in parenting. When it comes to discipline, children respond more quickly to males who follow through on the limits that are set. I recommend that both parents practice saying no. I remember being accused by grandparents of treating my young daughter like a dog because I insisted that we raise our voices when telling her no. As parents, my wife and I experienced no disciplinary problems with our daughter. As a result, she never had to be spanked. She knew immediately that we meant business and that we were there to follow through with consequences if necessary.

LIMITS

Teaching Limits

We should always teach our children about the limits we impose. They need to understand why we need rules in the world and what their responsibilities are in life. This should happen from an early age. When keeping our children from touching something hot, we say, "No! It's hot. It will hurt." We might tell a toddler not to pull the cat's tail because that will hurt it. Of course, the cat may use its claws or teeth to set a physical limit itself, much to the surprise of the youngster. Sometimes we learn through negative experiences, especially if they're painful.

It's always a good idea to post the rules of the house. No setting fire to the cat. No live-in boyfriends. No messing with Dad's favorite chair. No burning your little sister at the stake. No jumping off the roof onto the trampoline. No putting the goldfish down the garbage disposal. No cooking the pet rat in the microwave. No snakes or toads in the bathtub. No cherry bombs in the toilet. Just a few basic regulations imposed to prevent utter chaos.

On a more serious note, spelling things out for children is extremely important for them and for you as a parent. If it's down in black and white, it's much more difficult to dispute. You can and should engage your children in the process. This does not mean that they have veto power, only that they are allowed to have a say in how the house rules are structured. These rules are more likely to be followed.

This may mean allowing them to participate in establishing consequences for inappropriate behavior. As an example, the loss of privileges such as video games, a favorite toy, or their cell phone for a specific period of time may be appropriate. This does not mean that they have the ultimate decision-making authority, just input.

Consequences should be developmentally appropriate and related to the child's concept of time. Loss of a toy for a day is fitting for a five year old.

No video games for two to three days is long enough for a ten year old. Grounding until an adolescent is eighteen is generally non-productive and unenforceable—seriously, never go more than a week if you want it to work.

They also get to help in determining rewards for good behavior. They are given input but not the ability to dispute. Again, the younger the child, the sooner the rewards should come. Adolescents should be able to work toward long term goals, but young children need to be rewarded quickly and frequently. Arguing results in immediate consequences with no participation in the process. Parents decide, and that's final.

Structure is extremely important for children's development. They need to have rules to bang up against in order to gain an understanding and appreciation for structure in their lives. Setting those rules and responsibilities should be part of the game plan you establish with your spouse.

When we discuss discipline, limit-setting, and demands as parts of parenting, we need to understand the need for children to experience mild to moderate stressors in their lives. Children must be challenged if they're to grow physically, emotionally, and intellectually. Helping children find and push their limits is important in the development of resilience.

Research has indicated that stressors of moderate intensity, especially challenges that a young animal can manage or master successfully, may help that animal deal with later stress more efficiently and easily.[66] By studying monkeys, scientists determined that animals that had experienced earlier stress of a moderate degree secreted reduced amounts of stress hormones when stressed again. The prior-stressed monkeys functioned better socially, seemed less anxious, were more liable to explore their environments, and actually ate more than their non-stressed peers.

When evaluating Special Forces troops, researchers found them more "stress-hardy" than other soldiers. The Special Forces troops had taken part in "rigorous stress inoculation training" as part of the U.S. Army survival school. They found as well that the Special Forces troops displayed higher levels of a chemical that helped their brains regulate the stress hormones that are secreted in combat-like situations. Their brains came back to normal functioning much quicker than those of the regular troops.

Does this mean you should send your kids to the Rambo Preschool for Combat Training so that they'll be ready for kindergarten? No! I'm not recommending stress-induction training for our children, only emphasizing that an unchallenged child is less likely to do well under pressure. Overprotection and not allowing kids to experience challenges can make it more difficult to cope later in life.

> *"Too many people in leadership positions confuse leniency with compassion. They believe it is humane to lower standards and bend rules. Lower your guard, not your expectations. Open your heart to embrace those whose performances are deficient. Find the time to discover the root cause of their problem. Touch and inspire them to exceed their past results. Whenever leaders lower their standards, they're committing selfish acts."* **—Coach Lou Holtz**[67]

The same idea goes for kids. Set the standards high, but make them achievable. Reward effort, not necessarily perfect results. And always remember to enforce the limits in a fair and just manner, understanding what Bill Cosby said about justice: "The truth is that parents are not interested in justice. They just want peace and quiet."[68]

INSTANT REPLAY

- Never minimize the importance of discipline mixed with love.
- Disciplining children is always tough, but it is an essential part of parenting.
- Put enough emotion in your voice so that your children know you mean no first time you correct them.
- Setting limits is synonymous with setting standards.

- Educate your children about the limits you impose.
- Help your children find and push their limits because doing so is essential to the development of resilience.
- No arguing. Parents always have the final word.

> *"Without self-discipline, success is impossible, period."* **—Lou Holtz, the only football coach in NCAA history to ever lead six different programs to bowl games**[69]

CHAPTER 6

EDUCATION

Is It Really That Important?

"You should learn as if you were going to live forever, and live as if you were going to die tomorrow. Always be learning, acquiring knowledge and wisdom for that long journey ahead. Know that when you are through learning, you are through."
—*John Wooden*[70]

Education is thought to be the gateway to success in life. If you are well-educated, the opportunities for you in life are unlimited. At least this is the general perception of most people. Immigrants come to the United States in order to better themselves and ensure greater opportunities for their children. Education is consistently emphasized as a way to break out of poverty and to ascend the social ladder.

Education produces success in all areas of endeavor according to the most knowledgeable individuals in our society. Certainly this can be proven statistically, but is a formal education a true measure of success in life?

Are there other attributes or accomplishments that ultimately are more important than a Harvard degree? How many times a day do you quote Shakespeare, determine the length of the hypotenuse of a triangle, or refer to the capital of Outer Mongolia?

Is there a connection between basic "intelligence" as measured by intelligence tests and educational accomplishment? The answer to that question is *yes*. "Smart" people are more likely to go to college and obtain higher degrees.

It is easier for scholarly types to succeed in intellectual pursuits, so they may naturally go down this path.

There are notable exceptions to the notion that higher education is necessary for success. Bill Gates, a Harvard University dropout, created one of the most innovative and world-altering corporations ever developed. The programs he created for computers have altered the way the world functions on a daily basis. Was it his education that caused his success or his innate intellect coupled with a thirst for knowledge and the willingness to risk everything to accomplish his goal? Certainly, his early educational process enabled him to build upon his knowledge base. But he ultimately extended his understanding of the computing process to levels that allowed his innovations to become established.

Bill Gates made computer theory a pragmatic part of everyday life. He accomplished his goals, not because he sought education for education's sake, but because he wanted to apply his knowledge to everyday problems. Thomas Edison was not highly educated but applied principles of hard work and discipline to the process of inventing. He stated that "invention is 10 percent inspiration and 90 percent perspiration." Most often, these attributes are not taught in the classroom but are learned in the home environment. Parents are the ones who teach children about the values of hard work and discipline.

> *"Don't let schooling interfere with your education."*
> **—Mark Twain**[71]

When discussing education, many parents have difficulty understanding that to educate is more than teaching reading, writing, and arithmetic. Life instructs us every day if only we pay attention to what is going on around us. We certainly learn more by listening and observing than by talking and acting. We need to teach our children to be attentive to their surroundings and to understand that everyone around them contributes to their education.

> *"I never learned anything talking. I only learned things when I asked questions."* **—Lou Holtz**[72]

EDUCATION

Train your children to listen and question their surroundings. They will learn more this way than they could in a lifetime of formal education. Lifelong daily learning is essential for success, and it requires focus and attention. Not an easy process, it's based on discipline and hard work.

Teaching children to explore the world and question their understanding of their experiences sets the stage for a lifetime of learning. This may mean that the family vacation becomes a research project for the kids. They can become tour guides with the responsibility of discussing the topography, flora and fauna, and historic background of various stops along the trip. Make it fun. Who can come up with the weirdest obscure fact? Parents have to participate as well.

The great coaches recognize the importance of lifetime learning. Basketball coach Mike Krzyzewski emphasizes the need for self-education. "Continual learning is the key to effective leadership, because when you stop growing, you start to decay."[73]

If you are constantly questioning and examining yourself and your environment, then your children will incorporate the love of introspection and exploration into their lives. It's that modeling thing again; what a great gift you will bequeath to them.

As parents, we want the best for our kids. Unfortunately, when it comes to education, many parents take this to the extreme. They want the best preschool and the best private education that money can buy. Exclusive preschools claim that graduates of their programs are more likely to be accepted to Harvard University post-doctorate programs in nuclear physics. You can imagine the preschool's headmaster bragging, "When children graduate from our preschool program, they can go into pre-algebra classes and will have read the complete works of Shakespeare. Place your child with us, and they will excel."

All too often, too much emphasis is placed on academic accomplishment and admission to prestigious universities over educating the child to achieve success in life. *It ain't all about book learnin'.* It's about developing a lifelong thirst for knowledge from life itself. Many highly educated individuals fail because they can't apply their knowledge to everyday life. Many academic overachievers have difficulty interacting with others and therefore do not live up to their potential. It is essential that we parents do not overemphasize the acquisition of the "best education" and denigrate the importance of life's lessons.

Multibillionaire J.R. Simplot, who came from very humble beginnings, is a prime example of learning from life's experiences. Mr. Simplot quit school in 1923 at the age of fourteen, finding that buying and selling hogs was more rewarding than sitting in a classroom. Then he started growing potatoes. During World War II, he helped develop a process of drying potatoes and began providing them to our troops. He went on to develop phosphate mines to fertilize his potatoes and large ranching operations to produce beef, and ultimately financed Micron Technology, a computer chip manufacturer.

Mr. Simplot did not achieve success through formal education, but on a daily basis, he learned life lessons from those around him. This ability allowed him to achieve goals that few ever accomplish. Although he never attended college, he left millions of dollars to university programs. He graduated from the greatest university of all—a life of hard work and dedication to achieve his goals.

Our education system is run by educators. During their schooling, they had to endure tedious lectures, mandatory classes, and often irrelevant requirements to attain their degrees. This process has been identified as "necessary" to produce a "well-rounded individual" and a requirement for attaining a teaching certificate.

Many teachers, following their professors, believe that if students are to be well-rounded, they too must sit through long, dull lectures, love ancient history, and absorb and regurgitate meaningless facts. After all, "It was good for me, so it must be good for them." Never mind if that this method often teaches students to be turned off by education and to see learning as boring or non-productive.

During my experience in medical school, internship, and residency, it seemed to be imperative that we demonstrate our capacity to work for extended periods of time without rest—thirty-six hours on, twelve hours off. This was the standard schedule for many medical students and interns on clinical rotation.

Young doctors were to be educated in this manner because it had always been done that way.

The faculty and medical staff seemed to have the attitude that, if they had to endure this initiation rite, so should those who follow in their paths. It has only been in the past ten to fifteen years that medical educators have become enlightened by the evidence. Exhausted young doctors are prone to make serious errors, often resulting in injury and even death for their patients.

Unfortunately, some doctors continue to pull "all-nighters" and still try to work the next day. You would think we would learn, but many doctors keep the "tough-it-out" tradition.

Just like medical school traditions have been slow to change, so have the methods for instructing our children. The educational system as it now stands does not meet the needs of many children. Unfortunately, I am made aware of this frequently with the children and adolescents I treat. A high percentage of children drop out of school and lack the skills to succeed in our increasingly demanding work environment. Industries bemoan the lack of skilled workers, yet schools continue to emphasize courses that have little meaning or practical use for many of their students.

For those children who have the inclination and intellectual abilities necessary to absorb and appreciate courses on Shakespeare and ancient history, this is all well and good. However, the great majority of our children and adolescents simply don't care if Hamlet was a Danish prince or that Ulysses S. Grant succeeded Lincoln's vice president Johnson to the presidency.

TIME-OUT!

I want to make it very clear that I am not condemning all teachers. We have many dedicated and ground-breaking educators in the system. Unfortunately, it is an "educational system" and systems by nature resist change and innovation.

How do we make school relevant? Why can't we teach life skills in a way that incorporates certain educational principles yet maintains the pupils' interest? Some schools, including one in Idaho, have decided to take on this task.

Financial Education

A major deficit in schooling is seen in the area of real-life, everyday finance. Learning about money cannot start too early. A survey of two hundred high school students revealed that parents do not do a good job of teaching their kids about finances.[74]

This report graded parents on how they interacted with their children regarding money. Most of the resulting grades for the group were in the F range.

- Parents discussed credit and debt at least monthly only 30 percent of the time. Overall grade: F.
- Only 50 percent of their adolescent children had a checking account. Grade: F.
- Fifty-one percent of the students did not have a debit card. Grade: F.
- A little over 60 percent of the students did not work enough to earn their own spending money. Another F.
- Twenty percent of the students received a regular allowance for spending money and were allowed to establish a budget for themselves. Guess what the parents' grade was? F.

In other areas, parents did better. Those who helped their children:

- establish savings accounts (78 percent) earned a C;
- know something about the annual household income (74 percent) earned a C.

Parents who were awarded A minus:

- did not allow their children to have credit cards in their names; and
- did not allow their children to have car loans in their names.

It is interesting to note that most of the kids wanted sound financial information. They wanted to learn how to budget, how to use credit and debit cards, and how to use credit wisely. Single parents seemed to do better than married parents in discussing these issues with their children.

The experts advised that parents share the details of their monthly budgets with teenagers to help them understand the real-life, nitty-gritty issues of deciding on priorities for spending. When they go off to college, they will be bombarded with credit card offers and tempting purchases that are beyond their capacity to finance. Many college students drop out of school, not because they have academic difficulties, but because they get into financial trouble.

The financial experts suggest that you talk to your children about budgeting, credit cards, borrowing, and debt starting at the age of eight. An allowance linked to performance is felt to be a good idea. They warn against allowing kids to get out of doing the chore by saying they don't want the money. If they refuse to do the chore, they lose a privilege or their favorite toy for a week.

TIME-OUT!

One of my editors, Susan Thomas, recounted a personal experience illustrating the importance of including kids in the budgeting process.

"When my daughter Angela was in junior high and I was a single mom, I hired her to do the books for our household. Each month she'd tell me how we did the previous month: 'Deficit spending again, Mom, and the problems are the same as last month: clothing and entertainment.' I told her that, this way, she'd find out how a household should not be run. Must have been effective, as she is now a frugal business owner whose financial planner told her she's never seen anyone who saves as much of her income as Angela does. Makes me feel good!"

Professionals recommend that appropriate spending be encouraged. Kids need to learn how to shop and track their expenses. Opening a savings account is essential. They even suggest that the child go to the bank to make deposits. A certain amount from their allowance or spending money should be allocated to savings.

When they get old enough to drive, they need to understand the total expense of maintaining and driving a car. What does it cost to finance a car? How much money is spent on gas? How do they plan to pay for their parents' increased auto insurance rates because there is a teenage driver in the family? Making teens responsible for the increased cost of insurance helps them to understand that there is no free ride in life. Allocating part of their allowance for gas money can be a rude awakening to the costs of owning and operating an automobile. If you are responsible and accountable, you get to drive; if not, you don't. Driving is a privilege, not a right.

One charter school has taken the importance of teaching children financial responsibility to another level.[75] The school requires kids in kindergarten to be exposed to the economics of life in order to make them better consumers and help them understand the fundamentals of business. In kindergarten (that's right, as early as kindergarten), the children learn the difference between *wants* and *needs*.

In class, teachers create choices that instruct the students on how to determine what they actually need to live and what they might want but may not need. The teacher may hold up two scarves, one that is very expensive and beautiful, and another one that's plain but very warm. The kids are asked to determine why they need a scarf. If keeping warm is the purpose of a scarf, do they really need to spend double the price to stay warm? Do they buy the more expensive scarf just to say "mine is better than yours?" This is a great exercise for kids to go through every time they make a purchase.

The school teaches math by having kids balance a checkbook. They study how taxes are used to pay for services such as road maintenance, parks, and firefighters. Many adults think these services are free or that someone else pays for them. Insurance agents come into the classroom to talk about health-care and hospital expenses. The students earn Monopoly money from different jobs and practice paying expenses with their earnings. The introduction of real-life problems prior to leaving the protective and supportive family environment is likely to produce "dividends" later in their financial lives.

EDUCATION

For your children's well-being and your own peace of mind, it is important that you provide them with an understanding of what living in the real world requires. Very often, we prefer to shield our children from the daily worries of economic survival. Unfortunately, this does not prepare them for what they will face when they become parents themselves.

There is no reason why kids can't help pay bills when they are old enough. Have them help prepare the budget for the family. Explain all the deductions on your paycheck and where the money goes. It's a great way to apply their math skills and help them understand the family's finances.

We truly should support our children by modeling fiscal responsibility, setting limits on family expenditures, teaching them the basics of economics, and helping them understand that giving to others less fortunate is a moral/spiritual responsibility.

TIME-OUT!

> *If children understand that money the family could use is being deducted for government services, maybe they will demand governmental fiscal responsibility when they become adults. They need to make the connection early.*

Many experts decry the notion of giving money for grades. I don't. Some kids will work for money. Several inner-city schools have found that paying kids to attend school really works. As a parent, you may want to give a certain amount for an A, less for a B, and less for a C. Some kids will never be A-students, so make requirements for payment consistent with ability. Whatever you *pay them for grades* will be returned hundreds of times if they graduate.

The Fight Crime: Invest in Kids National Anti-Crime Organization, which is made up of over four thousand police chiefs, sheriffs, district attorneys, and violence survivors, found that high school dropouts are three and a half times more likely to be incarcerated than those who graduate. Seventy percent of inmates in the nation's prisons have not earned a high school diploma. The study estimated that three thousand murders and 175,000 violent assaults could be prevented if graduation rates were improved by only ten percent.[76]

"A child who graduates from school as a result of being paid for grades will give back ten-thousandfold in the form of taxes that they will pay as productive members of society. The resulting cost savings on welfare, healthcare, and prison expenditures will be enormous." —**Dr. T**

Parents who are involved in their children's schooling can make a huge difference. This is true even for disadvantaged kids. Parents can check on homework and help (within reason) with assignments. By displaying an interest, you send a loud and clear message that education is important. There will always be boring teachers and irrelevant classes, but the expectation is that your child will participate and will succeed.

Homeschooling has been gaining more adherents in recent years. This is certainly an option, especially if one parent can remain at home and is not required in the workplace. If this is not an option, it is important for parents to take an active role in their children's educational experience.

As we will see in the section on resilience and education, school districts are offering more job-related courses and should be commended. Vocational programs give students skills that will enable them to compete in the ever-changing job market.

Sex Education

Since there is a spiritual component to the S-M-I-L-E-S program, I reviewed the concerns of the major religions when it comes to sex education. Christianity, Judaism, and Islam emphasize delaying sexual activity until after marriage. The education experts of the various religious persuasions recommend that parents handle questions as they arise throughout a child's life.

Being a good role model and providing the example of a loving relationship are basic to helping children understand that sex is more than what they see on

EDUCATION

TV or hear from their friends. Having a thorough understanding of your individual religion's perspective on sex and marriage will allow you to be prepared when situations occur. Don't be afraid to ask for help. Consulting with your pastor, rabbi, or imam can be a first step. Talk with friends of similar persuasion for recommendations of sex education materials.

> "We have had 30 years of sex education in the secondary schools and it has never been easier for teenagers to get hold of contraception without their parents knowing, yet both abortion rates and sexually transmitted infection rates have continued to rise."[77]

Is this a comment on sex education in U.S. schools? No. The Family Education Trust in Great Britain was expressing concern about the 4,376 abortions given to girls younger than sixteen years of age in their countries. British legislators were appalled by the fact that Great Britain has the highest rate of teenage pregnancy in Europe. The controversy in England swirls around the teaching about sex in early elementary school, even as early as age four.

The Church of England expressed concerns about having sex education taught in a "morally neutral environment." The Church addressed the tendency to remove all reference to morality in the teaching of the biology of sex to students.[78]

The issue is no different in the United States and is perhaps more emotionally charged and divisive. Some groups[79] advocate extensive sex education programs starting in elementary school with the expressed goal of preventing pregnancy and sexually-transmitted diseases. They encourage teenagers to use contraception and emphasize the need for confidentiality for adolescents. These groups criticize programs advocating abstinence as being fear-based and ineffectual.

Those who support abstinence as the primary tool for pregnancy and disease prevention express concerns about the lack of parental involvement in these school-based programs. They are worried about the message these programs send to children and adolescents. Many religious groups are concerned that destigmatizing out-of-wedlock sexual activity will result in teenagers' engaging in sex more frequently, often with disastrous results.

TIME-OUT!

> *Similar concerns among different religions are plentiful. Writing online at themodernreligion.com, Shahid Athar, a Muslim concerned about sex education in our schools, quotes Father James Burtchaell, a Catholic priest: "Standard sex education today 'tends to be morally bankrupt. It begins with a biological description of sexual function and fertility ... and it ends with indoctrination in conception, abortion and venereal disease. Basic to this ... is the belief that youngsters will not accept moral ideals....'"*[80]

As a parent, you should be aware of the risks associated with unprotected sex. There are at least twenty-five different sexually transmitted diseases, which are the most frequently diagnosed infectious diseases in the American population. Approximately nineteen million Americans will develop a sexually transmitted disease (STD) in any given year, and almost half of those will be teenagers and young adults ages fifteen to twenty-four.

Unfortunately, most teens don't feel they are at risk and don't realize the seriousness of developing an STD. Viral infections such as herpes can be with a person for life, and the AIDS virus is potentially fatal.

Teenage girls are most at risk for complications because of the immaturity of their sexual organs. While bacterial and parasitic infections can be treated with medication, the diseases, even with treatment, have the potential for permanent damage and scarring, which can affect the young woman's fertility.

Teens are more prone to risky behaviors, and that risk-taking is multifaceted. If children or adolescents smoke, they're more likely to abuse drugs and use alcohol. Alcohol-using teens are seven times more likely to have had sex than those who do not drink. If teenagers use drugs, they are five times as likely to be involved in sexual activities.

Surprisingly, 53 percent of high school–age kids have not had sex, with 54 percent of the girls and 52 percent of the boys refraining from sexual activity.

Of those teenagers who do have sex, almost one-third of the girls will become pregnant and one in eight boys will have fathered a child. If their sexual activity starts early, before the age of fifteen, half of the girls will become pregnant.

Having more than two sexual partners increases the likelihood of pregnancy as well as the likelihood of contracting a sexually transmitted illness. In 2002, there were more than 750,000 teen pregnancies and 215,000 teen abortions in the United States.

Your teen does not have to be a statistic. You can make a difference.

Unfortunately, it is extremely difficult to protect young children from exposure to sexually explicit material. Billboards warning about AIDS and the condom display at the local mini-mart are constant reminders of how sex has pervaded our everyday lives.

Our daughters may idolize Hollywood celebrities, who are frequently self-absorbed young women whose morals, dignity, and use of drugs and alcohol are not appropriate for role models. Many of these famous women are products of the materialistic entertainment community whose mantra is "sex sells; and if you've got it, flaunt it."

Prime-time TV commercials advertise medications for erectile dysfunction, and even "family sitcoms" commonly allude to sex in objectionable ways. Shielding your children is next to impossible.

Most parents are concerned about how to bring up the topic of sex and how to determine if their son or daughter is listening. Often, parents were not informed by their parents. Not having role models makes it doubly difficult to discuss these issues openly.

Writing for the *Jewish Telegraphic Agency*, Jane Ulman describes her reaction to the question from her young son, who was studying sperm whales in school, "Just how does the sperm get from the male to the female?" (She states, tongue-in-cheek, that she always handles these issues with dignity, composure, and maturity.) "Larry," she shrieks to her husband, "get the book." (*Where Did I Come From?*) Their family had decided to have Dad deal with the issue of sex education as questions arose from their four boys. She goes on to state that had they been girls she would've been the one dealing with the issue.[81]

If parents are unwilling to "step up to the plate," information without their preferred moral content will be the basis of their children's understanding about sex. This will occur whether it is learned in the classroom or on the street corner.

Kids really want to know what their parents think about sex. Ninety-four percent of teens think parents should let teenagers know that they should wait to have sex until after they get out of high school. Eighty-eight percent of adolescents feel it would be easier to avoid early sexual activity if they had open and honest conversations with their parents. Believe it or not, almost 60 percent of teens say that their parents are role models for healthy and responsible relationships.

One survey found that two out of three teenagers who had early sexual intercourse wish they had waited. The great majority of children want their parents to help them set limits for themselves.

When it comes to sex education, the Internet opens up a wealth of resources to help parents. One Web site with extensive information can be found at 4Parents.gov. Some of the topics include:

- the importance of marriage;
- the importance of developing and maintaining a supportive relationship with your children;
- why you need to talk to your child about waiting and other statistics previously quoted;
- suggestions on how you might bring up the subject of sex and the best ways to initiate a conversation in a nonjudgmental and supportive fashion;
- how to teach your son or daughter to say no;

EDUCATION

- answers for tough questions;
- support for parents whose children have become sexually active;
- extensive explanations about birth control;
- even the options available should your adolescent become pregnant.

The 4parents.gov site is a basic, informational site with no moral bias. The moral part is for you as a parent to discuss. This certainly takes teamwork in coordination with your spouse. Keep the avenues of communication open with your child. Refer to the experts for help and information. Be open and honest about your concerns, and be sure to tell your children that you would like for them to wait.

TIME-OUT!

When it comes to watching TV excessively, inactivity and obesity are not the only problems. A study reported in the Archives of Pediatric and Adolescent Medicine[82] found an association between increased television viewing and the risk of early initiation of sexual activity by young adolescents. The researchers cited other findings that had found an association between the initiation of sexual activity by younger adolescents and "risky sexual behaviors, increased risk of multiple partners, unwanted pregnancy, sexually transmitted infections, and pelvic inflammatory disease."

The authors quoted several predictors of early sexual intercourse:

- early puberty
- poor self-esteem
- depression
- poor academic performance

- low parental education
- lack of religious participation
- lack of nurturing parents
- cultural and family patterns of early sexual experience.

The researchers found that "lack of parental regulation of television programming was associated with increased one-year risk of sexual initiation in these adolescents." The group determined that "the rate of initiation was highest among those who watched television two or more hours per day and had no content rules." In other words, they watched whatever they wanted to watch with no parental supervision or intervention. Monitoring your children is one of your key tasks as a parent.

Resilience and Education

Parents should expect their children's educational experience to foster resilience. Katie Frey, PhD, when writing about resilience in children, described several qualities necessary in schools to promote resilience in the children under their care. The school climate must provide a secure and positive learning environment. The emphasis should be on flexibility in teaching and building on student strengths. Success should be celebrated with both students and parents. Contact with supportive adults who can serve as mentors and role models should be the basis for teaching. A sense of trust, caring, and responsibility should be easily discernible throughout the school from the principal down to the janitor.

There should be certain expectations for the students and the staff. All students should be accepted unconditionally, recognizing both strengths and weaknesses, with the understanding they will be challenged to perform up to their potential. Staff and students should believe in the ability of every student and demonstrate the value of cooperation and helpfulness. Service to schoolmates and the community should be a mandatory requirement.

EDUCATION

Skills basic to developing resilience in the students should be emphasized. In addition to succeeding in academics, students' attainment of social competence and the ability to relate well to others should be integral to their learning process. Helping the children become self-motivated so that lifelong learning takes precedence in their lives is essential to their educational experience.

Critical-thinking, problem-solving, and decision-making skills should be integrated into the academic curriculum. Learning about cause-and-effect relationships has many applications in the real world environment. Innovative learning experiences building on the students' past knowledge should be emphasized. Identifying hidden talents and allowing children to learn in an environment where individualized learning styles are employed will engage children in the educational process.

In an ideal world, your child's school would be providing the educational environment for the production of a resilient well-educated child or adolescent. If your school system does not offer adequate services, it is your job as a parent to provide supplemental educational experiences for your child. You can create a learning environment that allows your child to develop the life skills necessary for success.

Remember that you need to advocate for your child. Make certain that your child's needs are being addressed and that the educational system is performing. This means that you as a dad go to parent-teacher conferences when possible, communicate with your child's teacher and work with the school to obtain services for your child. Support your child in every sense of the word.

INSTANT REPLAY

♦ Teach your children to be attentive to their surroundings and to understand that everyone around them contributes to their education.

♦ Constantly question and examine yourself and your environment to incorporate the love of introspection in your child.

♦ Do not denigrate the importance of life's lessons.

- Model fiscal responsibility.
- Learn to discuss questions about sex.
- Be a good role model—exemplify a loving relationship.
- Play an active role in your child's education.
- Advocate for your child.

> *"The eight laws of learning are explanation, demonstration, imitation, repetition, repetition, repetition, repetition, and repetition."* —***John Wooden***[83]

CHAPTER 7

YOU GOTTA BE A GUY:

(with apologies to Jeff Foxworthy)

Men and Shopping

> *"You gotta be a guy if your definition of an extended shopping excursion with your wife is a fifteen-minute trip to the auto parts store."*

When talking about shopping, men and women are in different universes. A research study called "Men Buy, Women Shop" was picked up by the *Wall Street Journal* in the December 14, 2007, edition. The article detailed the results of a telephone survey of 1,205 men and women. The researchers attempted to determine the different styles of shopping by gender. They found that men were more task-oriented, get-it-done, in-and-out shoppers. Women, on the other hand, liked to talk and wanted the salespeople to pay attention to them. They looked at shopping as an experience. For the guys, it was a chore.

The shopping experience was compared to the hunter versus the gatherer approach. As it turns out, men were more concerned about getting a parking space near the entrance of the store, whereas women wanted to spend time discussing their purchases with the store personnel. If women were turned off by the experience, they were more likely never to shop there again. Men were more forgiving.

A warning to young fathers:

If you have a daughter, expect her to become an expert shopper at a very early age. The urge to shop appears to be a sex-linked, hereditary phenomenon. I am certain that even girl infants presented with two clothing tags, one regular price and the other tagged 40 percent off, would choose the discounted one in a heartbeat.

Women are, as the article stated, "shopping queens." Statistics prove the author's point. Women account for 83 percent of all purchases in the United States. That's four trillion dollars' worth every year.

Men are left in the dust. It's like a Pop Warner football team playing the winner of the Super Bowl.

THIRD QUARTER

"A waist is a terrible thing to mind." —*Tom Wilson, comedian*

"Inside of us is a thin person trying to get out, but they can usually be sedated with a few pieces of chocolate cake." —*Author unknown*

"I have to exercise in the morning before my brain figures out what I'm doing." —*Marsha Doble, personal trainer*

CHAPTER 8

DON'T SAY DIET

Say Lifestyle Change

"You've got bad eating habits if you use a grocery cart at 7-Eleven." **—Dennis Miller, comedian and radio talk-show host**[84]

Food is a big issue for guys. Our moms stuffed us to the gills throughout our formative years. In most families, food means someone cares. Eating Mom's special apple pie with tons of ice cream is a way of accepting her love without getting all gushy. It's apparent that we continue to look to moms for sustenance long after we grow up and move away.

One example shows up on TV commercials where professional football players (almost all overweight) exalt hearty soups and stews being fed to them by one of their famous mothers. *Fill them up! Don't let those kids go away hungry! They're growing boys!*

Unfortunately, the commercials set up the expectation that you should be filled to the brim after every meal. *Stuff it in there! You never know when you're going to get your next grunts. You gotta eat big to be big!*

We've got a huge problem with obesity in this country, but you can be part of the solution. Here is where modeling becomes important. You and your spouse have to decide on what your game plan is for nutrition. This means sitting down and looking at your eating habits and food preferences.

"I come from a family where gravy is considered a beverage." —**Erma Bombeck, author**[85]

The high-calorie comfort foods you loved when you were growing up will need to be changed. This means blending the eating patterns of the two families of origin. Not an easy task, especially when her mother's coconut cream pie tastes so good! And you have always eaten the German chocolate cake that your mother baked for you on your birthday. Life without potatoes drowning in butter, sour cream, and bacon bits—impossible!

You're going to have to change your mindset from the clean-your-plate attitude about food to eating more healthy types and amounts of food. Unfortunately, most of the time, guys just want to eat what they like and expect it to be prepared and on the table when they get home. They give little thought to what they put in their mouths so long as it tastes good and there is plenty of it. Calories and fat content be damned! "Vegetables! Vegetables! I don't gotta eat no stinkin' vegetables!" Unfortunately, this is just unacceptable.

Overweight parents beget overweight kids. Do you want to condemn your child to a lifelong fight against obesity, problems with diabetes, heart disease, and other illnesses related to being overweight?

Think I'm kidding? Here are some startling statistics about the obesity epidemic in our kids. A study titled "Childhood Obesity: Are We Missing the Big Picture?" states that "obesity has become a leading cause of preventable morbidity and mortality worldwide."[86] Simply put: People get sick with hypertension, diabetes, arthritis, cancer, heart disease, and other ailments because they are overweight. Obese folks die at an earlier age.

It is estimated that worldwide 10 percent of school-age children are obese. Latin America leads the pack with 32 percent; Europe has 20 percent; and the United States, 17 percent. The obesity rate today is three times the rate it was thirty years ago. Nineteen percent of children ages six to eleven are obese, an increase from just 4 percent in 1971. One-third of all American kids are overweight, and 90 percent of the overweight kids have at least one risk factor for heart disease, which is totally avoidable. The direct and indirect annual costs from obesity are estimated to be approximately $120,000,000,000.

According to studies, children are eating lots of high-carbohydrate foods like potatoes, cereals, and sugary soft drinks. This goes along with the trend toward fast food, which now accounts for 30 percent of all meals for most families. A fast-food meal can contain more than 2,200 calories. That's a day's worth of calories for most people and would require a full marathon to run it off.

TIME-OUT!

My pet peeves are the sugary snacks in schools and the limited amount of physical education activities offered to our kids—only 25 percent of America's children have regular physical education. [87] *Parents need to push schools to incorporate classes to help kids understand the importance of diet and exercise.*

Look at the example of one educator, Principal Yvonne Sanders-Butler, who instituted extreme measures in her suburban Atlanta elementary school—she banned sugar. [88] *Since the sugar-free program was established ten years ago, there has been a 15 percent increase in students' standardized test scores as well as a 23 percent decrease in disciplinary problems. Along with being sugar-free, the program included daily exercise in the form of dancing and healthy food in the cafeteria with more fresh fruits and vegetables. Students' health improved and obesity was no longer a problem.*

Critics claimed the school's budget couldn't handle the change, while in fact the program has seen a savings of $425,000 over the past nine years. It is also remarkable that the kids like the program and even "rave about carrots and cauliflower."

Taking care of one's physical health is the foundation for learning and emotional health. Dr. Butler said it best, "For me it was not just educating children about reading, writing and arithmetic. If these people were going to be successful, I had to ensure that they were going to be healthy." [89]

It's an alarming fact that obese kids often have cardiac trouble. Dr. David Ludwig, director of the obesity program at Children's Hospital, Boston, found that the more overweight a child was between the ages of seven and thirteen, the greater the risk of heart disease in adulthood.[90] A normal thirteen-year-old boy has a 12 percent risk of developing heart disease as an adult, but a child the same age weighing twenty-five pounds more has a 16 percent chance, or a one-third increase.

Researchers studying members of a Mormon community who fasted one day a month for religious reasons found that they had lower rates of heart disease.[91] What if you fasted three or four days a month? Would you die? I don't think so. It takes well over a month to starve to death with no food whatsoever. Missing a meal or even three will not adversely affect a normal person's health.

When you read in the papers about hikers who become lost and go without food for two days, you may gasp in horror. This situation shouldn't alarm you, as you'd just be putting yourself into ketosis, which means you'd be burning fat. It's the basis of the low-carbohydrate, high-protein diets recommended to lose weight. You produce these wonderful compounds called ketones. When you're losing weight, they give you a sense of well-being and are a preferred energy source for the brain. You can get a sense of euphoria and lose weight at the same time.

> *"I drive way too fast to worry about cholesterol."*
> **—Steven Wright, comedian**[92]

Steven Wright may have one approach to solving this problem, but thankfully, American men are becoming more aware of developing healthy lifestyle habits. Guys are now being targeted by food and diet programs that used to be aimed toward women. "You too can lose fifty pounds and get back in the game," Dan Marino and the gang tout the benefits of the NutriSystem program. John Kruk, a rotund baseball commentator for ESPN, said, "I lost so much weight that my wife doesn't think I'm nearly as disgusting as I used to be." Even Larry the Cable Guy was able to drop fifty pounds from around his gut using the plan. If it works, go for it, but there are less expensive approaches than these packaged weight loss plans.

Numerous studies have evaluated various diet plans. One study reported in the *Journal of the American Medical Association* compared a low-fat, high-carbohydrate diet with the high-fat Atkins plan. The Atkins plan, which allows and even encourages the intake of fats and protein over carbohydrates and starches, seems to work better over the long term. People could stick with the Atkins plan and were able to keep the pounds off once they were lost.

> *"It's a scientific fact that your body will not absorb cholesterol if you take it from another person's plate."*
> **—Dave Barry, humorist and newspaperman**[93]

You don't have to continue down the road to obesity. You have the opportunity to prevent your child or children from becoming another statistic. It ain't easy, but you can do it. Just follow *Dr. T's Ten Tantalizing Lifestyle Tips for Looking Good and Feeling Good.*

Dr. T's Ten Tantalizing Lifestyle Tips incorporate the concept of limiting carbohydrates with the understanding that if food doesn't taste good you won't eat it.

1. Don't say diet. It's a lifestyle change. Weight loss is more than calorie restriction. It is a mindset and commitment.

2. Do it for you. You're the most important person in your life. You deserve to look good and feel good. This may sound all touchy-feely, but it's true. You are the person in charge of your life, and there isn't anyone who can change your eating habits for you.

3. Don't try to change too much at once. You didn't eat an extra piece of cheesecake one night and wake up to discover you gained forty pounds. It took time to put it on; it will take time to take it off.

4. If nothing else, increase your exercise. Even if you don't lose weight, you'll feel better. Guaranteed. This is tough. You must set aside time to do

something physical every day. Activity defeats fat every time. Remember that fact and act on it today. Walk! Walk! Walk! Start out with ten minutes and work up to thirty minutes a day. Start an upper-body exercise program when you have established the walking habit. (More on exercise in the following chapter.)

5. Notice what you eat and cut out the sugar and other refined carbohydrates. Look at what you drink. Did you know that there are a whopping 640 calories in four cans of soda pop? That's one "big gulp." If you cut out those sugar-filled drinks, you could shed 66.7 pounds in one year. Don't opt for fruit juice either; it's all sugar. Oranges, apples, and other fruits are great but not the juice alone. It takes five oranges to make 12 ounces of orange juice. You get all the sugar and little of the healthy fiber.

    Crystal Light is a no-sugar, fruit-flavored drink. It tastes fairly good and is a lot cheaper than diet pop in a can. As for beer—what can I say? Even the light, low-cal stuff has calories. Limit your consumption. It's called a beer belly for a reason. If you must drink alcohol, make it red wine in moderation. Red wine in moderation can be helpful in preventing heart disease. This is a personal choice, however, and there are many other factors that influence the development of hardening of the arteries. So don't tell your spouse Dr. T said, "It's okay to drink half a gallon of Boone's Farm because it's good for you."

6. Grandma was right. Eat your vegetables—stir fry is great. Believe me, leaving french fries out of your diet will not cause diabetes—or hair loss for that matter. Want a fry? Eat a carrot; watch the pounds fall away. If you must have a snack, raw veggies are great. Anything packed with water and fiber will fill you up but not fill you out—break out the celery, cauliflower, broccoli, baby carrots, bell peppers, and even sugar snap peas. Low-calorie salad dressing makes a good dip. Set the example!

7. Think lean steak, chops, chicken, hamburger, and fish (without the chips). Protein in any form is better than candy, cakes, or chocolate-chip macadamia-nut cookies. A hamburger without the bun and chicken tenders on a green salad are low-carbohydrate meals. Who said you had to give up fast food? Make a meat wrap. A slice of ham wrapped around a slice of low-fat cheese makes a good low-carb snack.

    Get a grill pan. Grill your protein. Be a healthy part of the cooking process. Your spouse will think you're being a great help. Use your outdoor grill year-round. I'll even give you a family secret. Dust your protein with a little seasoning (McCormick's, Tony's Louisiana Seasoning, etc.) and garlic powder to taste. Top it with olive oil and put it on the grill. It's easy, quick, and makes you a hero.

TIME-OUT!

Fry some bacon and save the grease to baste your meat while cooking. Freeze it in an ice tray for storing. Most of the fat burns off. You'll get lots of flavor with few calories.

8. Make the veggies taste good. They have to taste good, or you won't eat them. It's hard to overdose on butter. Do you remember ever seeing anyone lick a butter cube? Disgusting! If you do use butter, very little of it really sticks to the green beans or other vegetables. Butter makes veggies taste better but may not add that much to your calorie count. It's when you add a stick of butter and some sour cream to the mashed potatoes that the calories go through the roof.

    Make your salads taste good. All sugarless salad dressings in moderation will work. Olive oil with balsamic vinegar is great—easy to make and tastes good. Good for you, too!

9. If you must eat bread, make it multigrain or whole wheat. Use some butter (not the whole stick); you'll eat less bread. Better yet, try olive oil and some parmesan cheese. White bread is a no-no. It goes directly to the hips.

10. Our well-meaning mothers trained us to *clean our plates*. Eat all your starch, or you won't get your sugar-filled dessert. But remember, smaller portions mean slimmer waists. Having seconds or thirds is not a God-given right, so cut them out. If you must have dessert, go sugar-free (ice cream, Jell-O). Cheese, nuts, fruit, and dark chocolate in moderation are all good alternatives to that carbohydrate-filled piece of cake with cream cheese icing.

Snacking is a no-no! For whatever reason, whenever we feel hungry, we have to satisfy that urge to eat. It's very easy to sit down and eat a bag of chips and drink a sugar-filled soft drink or sugar-sweetened iced tea. You may feel you have to eat that piece of candy to give yourself a sugar boost, or to have three pieces of bread while waiting for dinner to be served. No wonder three out of four American men are overweight. What behavior are we modeling for our children?

Late-night snacking and overall high-caloric intake may even influence your sleep patterns. *Medscape Medical News*[94] reported a study in Brazil examining the correlation between late-night, high-caloric snacking with awakenings during the night similar to sleep apnea. The subjects in the study experienced more fragmented sleep and had periods during which they stopped breathing. Sleep apnea, a very dangerous and debilitating condition, is most often found in obese individuals. Takeaway message: Cut back, especially at night.

Incorporate the kids in meal planning and preparation. Help them learn how to cook for themselves when they grow older. Make meal preparation a family affair, and it will add to the enjoyment of dining together.

> *"I found there was only one way to look thin, hang out with fat people."* **—Rodney Dangerfield, comedian**[95]

I know you don't want to hear all this about your diet, but you need to pay attention for your kids' sake. A disturbing fact, reported in TIME magazine,[96] is that some parents don't recognize that their own children are overweight. One study found that only 36 percent of parents of overweight kids between the ages of twelve and seventeen identified their obese children as overweight.

Studies from Australia and England show that parents of younger children were even more likely to underestimate the problem. Fewer than 2 percent of British parents saw their three- to five-year-olds as obese, and only 11 percent of

Australians thought their five- to six-year-olds had a weight problem.[97] "They'll just grow out of it. It's only baby fat." Wrong!

Have your pediatrician regularly plot your child's body mass index (BMI—a measure considering both height and weight in determining obesity, which is more accurate than weight alone).Better yet, go online (http://www.nhlbisupport.com/bmi/) and get the whole family's results every three months.

If you don't have access to the Internet, here's the formula.

$$BMI = \frac{(\text{weight in pounds})}{(\text{height in inches}) \times (\text{height in inches})} \times 703$$

BMI Categories:

- Underweight = <18.5
- Normal weight = 18.5 – 24.9
- Overweight = 25.0 – 29.9
- Obesity = 30 or greater

Get out your calculator and remember what Miss Piggy said: "Never eat more than you can lift."

INSTANT REPLAY

♦ Cut out empty calories (sugar, carbs).

♦ Eat lots of veggies and fruit.

♦ Leave out the starch (potatoes, pasta, rice, bread).

♦ Increase protein (meat, fish, poultry, eggs, cheese, nuts).

♦ Don't sweat the fat (butter, olive oil, and dressings make veggies and salads taste good).

- Downsize the portions, and no seconds.
- Families who spend time together around the dinner table produce children who are less likely to have problems in life.

> *"I really believe the only way to stay healthy is to eat properly, get your rest, and exercise. If you don't exercise and do the other two, I still don't think it's going to help that much."* —**Mike Ditka,**[98] *second and only other person to win the Super Bowl as a player (Dallas Cowboys, 1972), assistant coach (Dallas Cowboys, 1974), and head coach (Chicago Bears, 1985)*
>
> *Note: Mike Ditka had to have bypass heart surgery before he changed his eating and exercise habits. Don't wait; start today!*

Australians thought their five- to six-year-olds had a weight problem.[97] "They'll just grow out of it. It's only baby fat." Wrong!

Have your pediatrician regularly plot your child's body mass index (BMI—a measure considering both height and weight in determining obesity, which is more accurate than weight alone).Better yet, go online (http://www.nhlbisupport.com/bmi/) and get the whole family's results every three months.

If you don't have access to the Internet, here's the formula.

$$BMI = \frac{(\text{weight in pounds})}{(\text{height in inches}) \times (\text{height in inches})} \times 703$$

BMI Categories:

- Underweight = <18.5
- Normal weight = 18.5 – 24.9
- Overweight = 25.0 – 29.9
- Obesity = 30 or greater

Get out your calculator and remember what Miss Piggy said: "Never eat more than you can lift."

INSTANT REPLAY

◆ Cut out empty calories (sugar, carbs).

◆ Eat lots of veggies and fruit.

◆ Leave out the starch (potatoes, pasta, rice, bread).

◆ Increase protein (meat, fish, poultry, eggs, cheese, nuts).

◆ Don't sweat the fat (butter, olive oil, and dressings make veggies and salads taste good).

- Downsize the portions, and no seconds.
- Families who spend time together around the dinner table produce children who are less likely to have problems in life.

> "I really believe the only way to stay healthy is to eat properly, get your rest, and exercise. If you don't exercise and do the other two, I still don't think it's going to help that much." —**Mike Ditka,**[98] second and only other person to win the Super Bowl as a player (Dallas Cowboys, 1972), assistant coach (Dallas Cowboys, 1974), and head coach (Chicago Bears, 1985)

> Note: Mike Ditka had to have bypass heart surgery before he changed his eating and exercise habits. Don't wait; start today!

CHAPTER 9

EXERCISE

An Eight-Letter Word

"I hated every minute of training, but said, 'Don't quit. Suffer now and live the rest of your life as a champion.'" —**Muhammad Ali, American boxer and former three-time World Heavyweight Champion**[99]

Exercise is an eight-letter word. The way people avoid it you would think it's comparable to its four-letter brethren—to be banished from polite conversation. We think about exercise in our yearly resolutions, but then we seclude it into the furthest reaches of our minds, hoping it will stay tucked away for another 365 days.

Exercise is great, but what does it have to do with raising kids? One word: prevention. If you as a father can help your children develop the habit of regular physical exercise throughout their lives, you will have given them a gift of health and wellness beyond measure. You can be part of the solution rather than contribute to the problem.

The best way to get your kids off the couch is for you to set the example. This means developing a plan and demonstrating through your own behavior the importance of exercise in everyone's lives. To see Dad getting up every morning and getting on the exercise bike or taking a walk will do more to instill the need for exercise than twenty lectures on the importance of maintaining fitness. You are the example and need to be the leader in this area. Inactive, sedentary parents beget inactive, sedentary kids.

Go online to any number of health-related sites, and you will find advice to get you going. The Mayo Clinic Web site[100] provides information and advice on getting children turned on to physical activity. Another excellent Web site is KidsHealth.org.[101] This site discusses the benefits of regular exercise for children. Physical activity helps them develop stronger muscles and bones and leaner body mass. Exercise reduces obesity and the risk of type 2 diabetes, lowers blood pressure and blood lipid levels, and creates a better outlook on life.

Mary Gavin, MD, who reviews the exercise programs for KidsHealth.org emphasizes the need for children to develop endurance, strength, and flexibility. Aerobic exercise such as bicycling, in-line skating, soccer, basketball, walking, jogging, running, or tennis should be incorporated in any exercise program for kids. The site includes a section on fitness for kids who don't like sports, which makes the point that organized sports probably should not include preschoolers. Strength training can be part of a young child's daily exercise program. Doing push-ups and sit-ups with Mom and Dad is a way of integrating strength conditioning into a daily exercise routine. If you're really feeling brave, you can do push-ups with a small child on your back. Check with your doctor first.

KidsHealth.org recommends an hour of exercise a day for most children if there are no physical handicaps. Show your children you are concerned about exercise by taking the stairs, parking some distance from the store, and not wasting gas trying to find a parking spot in front of the restaurant.

Why is it that something so good for us is so hard to do on a regular basis?

Maybe it was those wind sprints we had to run for punishment after not giving our all in practice. Maybe it is society's goal of making our lives easier by reducing the physical work we have to do on a daily basis. We certainly don't have to go out and plow the fields or harvest and store the crops. No more hauling water for washing and cleaning, chopping wood for heating, or taking the horse-drawn wagon to town once a month for provisions.

Physical exertion is no longer in the equation. We now have dishwashers, vacuum cleaners, central heating and cooling, power-driven lawn mowers, electric hedge trimmers, and gas-guzzling minivans.

EXERCISE

Maybe there's a vast political, industrial, societal conspiracy to ultimately control our lives by making us flabby and out of shape. The conspiracy may be working like this: You sit in your nice comfy easy chair watching NASCAR while stuffing yourself with chips and dip. Your eyes are glued to the screen with commercials pushing you to purchase the latest labor-saving convenience. Green with envy that your neighbor now has a turbocharged, candy-apple red riding mower with power steering and four-wheel disc brakes, you're succumbing to the subliminal thought control that is subtly influencing your purchasing decisions.

You now find yourself forty pounds overweight, out of breath after walking up a flight of stairs, unable to play with your children for fear of hurting your back, and purchasing a leather punch to put new holes in your belt. Now, ripe for the picking, you have fallen into the trap. The machines that have been planning to take over the world and subjugate the human species are ready to strike. But you can get out. You can reverse this doomsday scenario.

You do not have to resign yourself to a life of inactivity and gluttony. You can save the world for future generations, but you must act now. Not tomorrow, not next month, not when you have time, but now. Get out of your chair and do a push-up. Walk across the room and back. If you can do these things, you will have taken your one "small step for mankind." We can't let the machines win. We have to take a stand. We need your help! Do it today! Do it for your country, and for your children and their children. We're counting on you. Don't let us down! Go before you become another victim of their treacherous plot. Exercise!

Over the last fifty years, society's values have changed with regard to eating and physical work. The number of calories ingested by an average person has increased by 1,000 calories a day, and the average calories burned per day has decreased by 700.[102]

Menial, physical labor is considered beneath us. The United States is flooded by immigrants legal and illegal willing to take the jobs most Americans feel are "too hard and backbreaking" for real Americans to perform.

The ideal occupation is now sitting in front of a computer screen, exercising only our fingers and brains. We drive to work, take the elevator to our office, send out for lunch, drive home picking up fast food on the way, sit down and eat in front of the TV, and then go to bed. Not exactly a vigorous physical workout. No wonder the fitness level of our population continues to decline and the epidemic of obesity accelerates.

We can blame it on society, but where is personal responsibility and accountability?

As a father, it is important that you take on this responsibility. You can be in charge of exercise for the family. You will need to work with your spouse, but this is your area to develop and manage. You may not be able to cook as well as your wife, but you can organize and innovate when it comes to developing a family exercise plan.

Why is it important to exercise? Because we humans are built to move. A baby starts moving before it is born, and young children are constantly in motion. As children, adolescents, and adults, we explore our environments through movement, ever expanding our ranges and experiences. In the prehistoric past, movement was necessary for gathering food, finding a mate, and establishing territory. Without movement, ancient peoples would have perished. Our brains are programmed to respond to physical activity by establishing new connections and even growing new brain cells. This makes sense because we need to establish new brain-cell connections to incorporate our exploratory experiences into our memories.

Our brains also reward us for exercising by producing endorphins that give us a sense of pleasure not unlike some of the drugs that humans abuse. This pleasurable experience is the "natural high" that runners and other athletes experience during and after exercise. As a psychiatrist, I recommend exercise to all of my patients to help with depression, anxiety, and stress. Exercise is the best anti-depressant! You feel better and look better when you exercise. Completing a workout gives you a sense of competence and accomplishment. It helps with your self-esteem and boosts your ego.

> *"I run on the roads long before I dance under the lights."* —**Muhammad Ali**[103]

EXERCISE

There are many exercise benefits, especially when it comes to chronic illnesses. Exercise is part of a regimen to prevent and treat many physical maladies. Heart disease is one of the leading causes of death and disability in the United States. It is preventable. Elevated cholesterol and fats in the blood called lipids are associated with heart disease. Exercise reduces those fats and bad cholesterol in the circulation and increases good cholesterol, which is associated with cardiac health. This is a two-for-one result just from taking a walk every day.

If you have a family history of diabetes and high blood sugars but don't know what to do, guess what, you should exercise! People with type 2 diabetes, the kind you get from being overweight, can be cured with regular exercise and weight loss. The operative word is *cured*. It will go away. High blood pressure is another reason people develop heart disease. By conditioning your heart and blood vessels through regular exercise, high blood pressure can be prevented. Those on medication for high blood pressure can reduce and at times eliminate pills simply by starting an exercise and weight loss program.

Weight loss and exercise are the keys to achieving success and preventing or improving the outcomes of other illnesses. Regular exercise has been shown to improve arthritis and to prevent osteoporosis (the thinning of the bones as we get older). If you are out walking and exercising, you are stressing your cartilage, bones, and ligaments, making them stronger. Studies show that individuals who exercise regularly are less likely to develop certain cancers.

Obesity is a killer. It is associated with the increased likelihood of early death from almost all causes. The lack of exercise and obesity go hand in hand because all the calories you don't utilize through exercise and growth will be deposited as fat. Exercise defeats fat every day.

Physical exercise sharpens your mind and allows you to focus better. Exercise will give you energy and even improve your sex life. Men who exercise are much less likely to suffer from erectile dysfunction. It improves your circulation to certain crucial areas and enhances your ability to enjoy physical intimacy.

Regular exercise can be essential for a good night's sleep. You may fall asleep better because there is a natural dip in body temperature after exercise, according to a report from the Mayo Clinic.[104] Exercise can be fun. Playing golf, playing tennis, going for a walk, playing catch with the kids, and gardening all can be enjoyable. Of course, check with your doctor before starting any exercise program.

Some kids can go overboard with exercise. The June 23, 2008, edition of *TIME* magazine devoted a double issue to "Our Super-Sized Kids." The article "Fit at Any Size"[105] states that as many as ten million women and one million men in the U.S. suffer from an eating disorder. Most of these individuals exercise to excess in order to lose weight. The KidsHealth.org Web site discusses compulsive exercise and how to identify the problem. It does no good to start exercising if you can't stop.

Modern conveniences such as televisions, DVD players, and computers have drastically affected the lives of children and families. If you're sitting on the couch watching TV or are going online to chat with a friend, you are less likely to be physically active. This lack of physical exertion has in part contributed to the epidemic of childhood obesity, type 2 diabetes, and general flabbiness in our children.

Most experts agree that this trend is only going to get worse if we don't get families involved in changing their attitudes toward exercise.

Until recently, type 2 diabetes accounted for only 5 percent of all childhood diabetes cases. Today 45 percent of all new cases of diabetes in children are now of the type 2 variety. These findings were reported in the *Archives of Pediatric and Adolescent Medicine*.[106] The researchers found that the number of hours television was watched on a school night and the number of soft drinks consumed per day were significantly associated with increased weight gain. Those who watched two or more hours of television had 5 percent more body fat and were 80 percent more likely to have a higher overall body mass index (BMI).

Researchers at the University of Buffalo Department of Social and Preventive Medicine found that by restricting TV viewing and the snacking that accompanied this activity, they were able to show a reduction in the BMIs of children over time. They reported that much of the snacking was related to commercials targeting young children.[107]

Another study[108] found that if parents were overweight, their children were likely to be overweight as well. Watching more TV just caused the problem to be worse.

There is a tendency for problems with weight to run in families. If a parent, especially the mother, is overweight, the children are 70 percent more likely to be overweight. If there is a tendency to be overweight in your family or your spouse's family, it is extremely important to monitor physical activity in your children and reduce TV watching to a minimum. The number of hours of TV viewing is increased dramatically if a child has a TV in his or her room. Having a personal television is not in the children's bill of rights.

Parents need to limit TV time and video-game time as an important part of setting limits for children. Computers can be used in the family area for homework. Some video games incorporate physical activity, which may be counted toward activity time.

TV Commercial

"Use our revolutionary abdominal toner for rock-hard six-pack abs in just five minutes a day. Buy the even faster six-minute workout, and you too can look like Arnold in his prime."

NO! NO! NO! If keeping fit and losing weight were so easy, I wouldn't have to include this chapter in the book.

Setting a routine time for exercise or play is essential. You need to schedule your exercise and set a regular time for your children to exercise daily. Make it a family affair. The family who walks together gets healthy together.

TIME-OUT!

> *If necessary, wear a backpack to increase your resistance. Add extra weight by carrying canned goods from the pantry or plastic bags filled with sand or dirt. Buy some light-weight dumbbells (5–10 pounds) to carry in each hand or use weighted straps that fit on your wrists and ankles. Weight on your extremities gives you more of a workout. Find a hill or several flights of stairs and watch your pulse rate climb along with you. So, no excuses—you don't need an athletic club membership or expensive equipment. Walk, walk, walk.*

Scientific evidence shows that walking not only improves you physically but also enhances brain function. Researchers divided stroke victims into two groups. One group walked on a treadmill three times a week, and the other group did stretching exercises during the same time frame. The walking group improved their speed on the treadmill by 51 percent and their cardiovascular fitness by 18 percent. The stretching group only saw an 11 percent improvement in fitness and a worsening, by 3 percent, of aerobic capacity.

"So what?" you might say. If you train, you get better. What the researchers found by using magnetic resonance imaging (MRI) of the participants' brains was that the walking group developed new circuits in their brains in areas that the researchers had not previously thought to be involved in exercise. The brain was actually attempting to heal itself and compensate for those deficiencies caused by the stroke. Astounding! If walking can do this for a damaged brain, what must be happening in our normal brains when we engage in physical exercise?[109]

The American College of Sports Medicine and the American Heart Association review thousands of scientific studies on exercise. These experts recommend a minimum of thirty minutes a day of moderate aerobic exercise like brisk walking.

Strength training should be included in the workout twice a week. This amount of exercise is maintenance. If you need to lose weight, the Centers for

Disease Control and Prevention (CDC) says sixty to ninety minutes of exercise may be necessary to take it off and keep it off.

Establishing the exercise habit is the most important part of the process. Pick a time, any time, and start. Some like mornings. It's a great way to start the day. You'll feel more refreshed and be more efficient. The late riser may want to exercise after work to wind down. If you take a walk at lunch, you may eat less.

Inclement weather? No excuses! We have wonderful inventions like hats, gloves, waterproof jackets, and umbrellas. Another option is to drop by the local mall and walk inside. No fair using the escalator—attack those stairs!

Establish the habit and do it for thirty days. I think you will never look back.

As for the kids, make it fun. Let them decide what type of activity works best for them. The more control you give them in selecting, the better they will participate in the activity. Every kid is different, but activity is what counts. You set the example as a "gold-medal" dad.

INSTANT REPLAY

♦ Start slowly and gradually increase your routine.

♦ Model being active with your children.

♦ Schedule regular exercise for your kids.

♦ Supervise and limit television time.

♦ Park some distance from your destination.

♦ Take the stairs rather than the elevator.

♦ Advocate for physical education classes in your kids' school.

- Exercise, exercise, exercise.
- You will feel better and look better when you exercise. Guaranteed.

*"You have to be willing to out condition your opponents." —**Paul "Bear" Bryant, Alabama football coach**[110]*

CHAPTER 10

FAILURE AND A POSITIVE ATTITUDE

The Capacity to Adapt

"If at first you don't succeed, you're running about average." **—M.H. Alderson, newspaper editor and publisher**[111]

You might wonder what failure and a positive attitude have to do with raising kids. Plenty! If you can help your children develop an optimistic view of life, you will have given them a gift that can stay with them forever. They'll have the ability to wake up eager to attack the problems they will encounter with optimism and enthusiasm. What an inheritance—an attitude that allows them to live life to the fullest every day!

Although we seek perfection, we rarely achieve it. We all fail on a daily basis. Failure is part of life. How we deal with failure is what's important and is a measure of our capacity to adapt. Failure puts our courage and tenacity to the test. As parents, we want the best for our children. We hope and pray they will be successful and at times push them excessively to achieve success. We may become upset when they do not meet our expectations. Looking at our own achievements in life, we may, at times, find them wanting. We want our children to exceed our own successes in life, and sometimes, we set the bar too high.

Our own expectations for ourselves become intertwined with the expectations we have for our kids. This may cause disappointment and a sense of failure for both us and our children. We all have seen the parents who are living out their desires for success through their children.

We only have to look at sports to understand that failure is the rule rather than the exception.

- A big leaguer gets a multimillion-dollar contract with a batting average of .333. That means that two out of three times he's at bat, he fails to get a hit.
- In a hockey game, there can be forty to fifty shots on the goal, but the team is doing well if they score three or four times.
- In basketball, if a team is averaging 50 percent from the floor, they are doing well.
- If the football quarterback completes 70 percent of his passes, he has had an outstanding day. But he had receivers making exceptional catches and an offensive line that kept him from getting knocked on his behind in order to accomplish this feat.
- When pitchers pitch a perfect game in baseball, they do not achieve perfection because they have to rely on faultless fielding from the rest of the team to get the twenty-seven up, twenty-seven down results. For the pitcher to get sole credit for a perfect game, he would have had to throw eighty-one pitches, all of which were strikes, and this has never happened in the history of major league baseball.

You can't hit a home run every time at bat, nor will you make every three-point basket at the buzzer. Dads have to step back and help their children deal with the inevitable failures they will experience by allowing failure to take its course. Kids will crash and burn when they are learning to ride a bike, skateboard, ski, and even walk, for that matter. We cannot eliminate adversity and pain from our children's lives, but we can assist them in working through the process.

Coach K has observed how parents view failure even at the collegiate level: "I think some parents now look at a youngster failing as the final thing. It's a process, and failure is part of the process."[112] Mike Candrea, University of Arizona women's softball coach, said, "How a player deals with the failure that is built into the game eventually determines how successful they will be."[113]

FAILURE AND A POSITIVE ATTITUDE

It is important to instill an attitude in our children that allows them to make mistakes knowing they can overcome adversity through perseverance. Helping our children understand that adversity is to be cherished not avoided can help them establish an attitude that will carry them to success.

> *"Success is never final, failure is never fatal. It's courage that counts." —John Wooden[114]*

We must model the courage to continue fighting and attack adversity rather than shun it. Demonstrating this capacity in our lives will help our children to develop a never-give-up attitude. Vince Lombardi recommended, "Learn from failure: failure can bring some of the toughest questions of all. If you answer them fully and honestly, you may learn more from failure than you do from success."[115] Coach Lombardi goes on to say, "It's not a failure if you learn something. Whether it's pain, mistakes, or success, every experience can teach you something. Sometimes the hardest lessons are the most important."[116]

When we understand that learning from experiences—no matter how difficult—is something to be cherished, we can assist our children in putting a positive spin on life. Lou Holtz said, "I think everyone should experience defeat at least once during their career. You learn a lot from it." He goes on to state, "You have to wait and see. I believe most problems are blessings in disguise. You can transform any tragedy into a positive experience simply by altering your perspective. Besides, the bad times are relative."[117]

How important is this positive attitude stuff anyway? It's all in your head. It really doesn't make any difference in real life, does it? Wrong—no, *big-time wrong*!

Researchers tell us that those individuals who have a positive outlook on life live 7.5 years longer on average. They found that having a positive attitude beat out low blood pressure and low cholesterol (four extra years of life) and not smoking and exercise (one to three extra years of life).[118] Not bad for looking at the glass as being half full rather than half empty.

We now have scientific evidence of changes in our brains associated with a pessimistic view of life. Researchers studying depression have been able to demonstrate abnormalities of a brain chemical called serotonin in pessimistic individuals. These abnormalities occur in the front part of the brain, the part that controls our thought processes. It shows that there is a biological basis for pessimistic thinking in depressed individuals.[119]

Children who are depressed are often very pessimistic. They will make statements like "I'm stupid," "I'm ugly," or other self putdowns. If your child is frequently negative and doesn't seem to be able to see the bright side of things, he or she may be suffering from depression. Recognizing depression in children and obtaining help early on can prevent significant suffering for the child as well as the family. Depression and other psychiatric conditions will be discussed more completely in the chapter titled "When Nothing Else Works."

In addition to increasing your life span, a positive attitude has been identified as being important in dealing with many medical illnesses and behavioral conditions. The "can do," positive approach helps your recovery from cancer, heart attack, and stroke. It is an important component of programs to stop smoking and fight obesity.

We all can get into negative thinking patterns that make it hard to feel positive about life. It is crucial to recognize these patterns in ourselves as well as in our families.[120]

Some people *blow things out of proportion*. To use a psychological term, they *catastrophize*. The smallest slight from a friend or a casual remark from a teacher brings the world down on us or our child. Everything becomes a calamity. The sky is falling, the world is coming to an end, and all because I didn't get the promotion or my child got a poor grade on a test.

FAILURE AND A POSITIVE ATTITUDE

> *"Seeing every disappointment as a catastrophe is not compatible with a positive attitude. Recognize that and eliminate it!"* —**Dr. T**

Filtering is another way negativity can creep into your life. You magnify negative aspects of what you have done rather than putting them in perspective. You or your child may have done a masterful job on a presentation, but because there may have been a minor slipup on a point, you focus on the small negative. You can't take or give yourself credit for the excellent job you did overall. You filter out a little imperfection for scrutiny and repeatedly berate yourself for your failure.

> *"Stop it, now! Accentuate the positive."* —**Dr. T**

Negative-thinking people often personalize events. If something bad happens, they tell themselves, "It must be my fault." If a trip or a party gets canceled, it's because "my friends don't want to be around me."

> *"Cut it out! You are not always at fault."* —**Dr. T**

Negativity can express itself in black-and-white thought patterns. This is called *polarization* and occurs when a person can't understand that the world operates mostly in the shade of gray. Events are rarely all good or all bad but somewhere in between. Persons who polarize have to do everything perfectly or they consider themselves total failures.

> *"Black-and-white thinking is unrealistic! Accept that life is not that clear cut."* —**Dr. T**

Negativity breeds negativity. The family environment you provide for your children can shape their attitudes for a lifetime. It is essential that you communicate with your spouse and ask for feedback. It's easy to fall into some of these negative thought patterns, but like any behavior, they can be changed. It's a matter of identifying them, changing the negative thought into a positive one, and practice, practice, and more practice. *I am absolutely positive that you can do it.*

Here are some examples of how you can alter your thought patterns.[121]

Negative Thought	Positive Alternative
I haven't done this before.	What a great learning opportunity.
This is overwhelming.	I'll just break this into little chunks and get it done.
This can't work.	I'll do my best to complete the project.
No one ever consults me.	I'll make sure to talk with everyone.
They always expect too much of me.	They must think I'm up to the challenge.
There's not enough time to get it done.	If I prioritize things, we'll make it happen.

Help children understand that the adversity they encounter in their lives may not be catastrophic by placing their life situation in context with that of others less fortunate. This can help them understand that the problems they encounter are surmountable. Growing up in adversity may be why many first-generation Americans achieve success. They have firsthand knowledge of a world in which being free to achieve is either more difficult or impossible.

Children who complain about not having the latest video game or brand-named clothes can write a report on Haiti or some other impoverished country. Better yet, they can spend a week wearing the same set of clothes like kids do in third world countries.

Today's Serbian tennis players are among the best in the world. They grew up in a war-torn country. Ana Ivanovic, who became the number-one woman in the world, had to practice in an empty swimming pool during the war. There is always someone around the globe who has it worse than you. So stop feeling sorry for yourself and get it done.

Even Abraham Lincoln looked at the possibility of failing when embarking on his quest to free the slaves and save the Union. He commented, "The probability that we may fail in the struggle ought not to deter us from the support of a cause we believe to be just."

Fear of failure can be the greatest hindrance to success. We all have to overcome our fears in order to exist in an ever-changing world. We have to help our children understand what Billy Joel said: "You're only human. You're supposed to make mistakes." According to John Wooden, "If you're not making mistakes, then you're not doing anything. I'm positive that a doer makes mistakes."[122] Hang in there and understand that failure is part of success. Enable your children to learn from your modeling.

> *"Nothing would be done at all if we waited until we could do it so well that no one could find fault with it." —John Henry*[123]

We must teach our children not to be embarrassed by attempting something and being unsuccessful. Young children do not think about failure until they are taught to fear it. When toddlers are learning to walk, they think nothing of falling a hundred times before walking across the room. It is the parent who becomes frustrated when the spoon full of carrots misses the baby's mouth for the tenth time during the learning process. The baby is not worried about cleaning up the mess or getting food on its face but only wants to get the spoon in its mouth, hopefully with some of the pureed carrots on it. It's parents who are uptight, not kids.

> *"If you don't think you can do it, then you certainly won't." —Dr. T*

Helping our children develop a positive attitude is key to ensuring their ability to deal with life's travails. Coach Holtz, in his book *Winning Every Day*, emphasized the importance of a positive attitude: "Life is 10 percent what happens to you and 90 percent how you respond to it."

The sports psychologist Jim Loehr, when describing the positive attributes of successful athletes, said, "The ability to summon positive emotions during periods of intense stress lies at the heart of leadership."[124]

We want our children to be leaders, whatever their goals in life might be. Instilling a positive attitude in our children, especially when dealing with difficult problems, will enable them to live up to their potential.

A positive attitude includes our feelings about ourselves. If you don't believe in yourself, it is hard to succeed. Iron Mike Ditka said, "Before you can win, you have to believe you are worthy."[125] Helping our kids understand that they are worthy and capable is essential for their success.

> *"I am the greatest!" —**Muhammad Ali**[126]*

> *"It's not bragging if you can back it up." —**Muhammad Ali**[127]*

Some people like to play the blame game. We see it all the time in sports, politics, and life. Yogi Berra, poking fun at himself, said, "I never blame myself when I'm not hitting. I just blame the bat, and if it keeps up, I change bats. After all, if I know it isn't my fault that I'm not hitting, how can I get mad at myself?"[128] If Yogi did get mad at himself, he would have said, "I made a wrong mistake."[129]

We all do it. "If it weren't for the weather, if I'd had more sleep, if the sun had not come up, if it wasn't freezing at the South Pole, everything would have gone much better." Politicians are very good at blaming others. You often hear them complain about how the press distorted this or that and how the media don't focus on the positive and blow things out of proportion.

FAILURE AND A POSITIVE ATTITUDE

In sports, we often see players do the same thing. They blame something or someone other than themselves for their bad performance. In tennis, even at the professional level, we see players looking at their rackets after they hit the ball out. Are they thinking that it must've been that string that was out of place? No, *it was the frame. Maybe if I bang it on the court really hard, that will fix it. Maybe if I yell at the umpire, who gave me a bad call three games ago, it will make things go better. Everybody is against me: the ball boys, the trainer, even the fans. That's why I hit the ball out, or was it even out?* Take responsibility for your behavior and don't blame others.

> *"Don't blame other people. Don't burden other people with your complaints. Ninety percent of the people you meet don't care about your troubles, and the other ten percent are glad that you have them."* **—Lou Holtz**[130]

There appears to be scientific evidence that Coach Holtz is right. A research study evaluated a group of teenage girls and boys who vented to each other about their problems. It was concluded that excessive venting not only was draining to those around them but did not contribute to problem solving. Moderate discussions of frustrations appeared to establish closer relations between females, but excessive discussions made things even worse.[131]

It's interesting to note that there was a difference between male and female respondents. Researchers found that men did not analyze their feelings or relationships as extensively as women did. Like in the commercial, the guys' venting may have been related to studying the emptying characteristics of beer cans more than talking to each other about their girlfriends.[132]

As we will see in the chapter on resilience, having a positive attitude has been found to be associated with emotional resilience. Optimism and a sense of humor have been found to improve resilience and result in greater life satisfaction. People who have a positive approach to life are less likely to develop mood disturbances, to use medical services, and to succumb to stress-related illness.

An article in *Prevention* magazine[133] illustrates what a positive attitude can mean in a person's life. The story of Angela Madsen, who became partially paralyzed from the waist down after surgery, is inspirational. Angela's weight increased to more than three hundred pounds before a doctor told her that her physical condition was "a waste of a human life."

The doctor's remark caused Angela to change her attitude dramatically. The forty-seven-year-old single mother and grandmother changed her feelings of hopelessness to feelings of accomplishment and success through sports. She won awards for surfing, basketball, swimming, rowing, and weight lifting, and at the time the article was written, she was preparing to row across the Atlantic Ocean alone.

Psychiatrist Steven Wolin, MD, is quoted in the article: "It's easy to blame other people for your problems and wait until they fix them. Unfortunately when you have a negative attitude you're unlikely to rise to the occasion and witness your own strength. If you think of yourself as a problem solver, life goes very differently."[134]

> *"The expectation of success is rarely the prelude to failure. The expectation of failure is almost always the harbinger of disaster."* **—Dr. T**

> *"Failure is not fatal, but failure to change might be."*
> **—Coach Wooden**[135]

As a father, you should look at your behavior and think, *What can I change to become a more positive role model for my children? How can I instill in them a more positive outlook toward life and the future?* The best way to reinforce their willingness to try new things is to accept their small failures as part of the process of mastering a task. Don't expect perfection, but encourage progress toward the goal.

Coach Holtz summed up the responsibility all parents have to their children: "As a leader, your attitude has a powerful impact on others. You have an obligation to develop a positive attitude, one that inspires people around you to achieve the impossible." He goes on to say, "You must have self-confidence in order to compete. I don't care what you do, never question your ability. Do everything you can to improve your performance, but when game time comes, take the field thinking you are the best."[136]

Coach Holtz emphasized the need for preparation and falling back on the basics. This speaks to the importance of repetition, repetition, and more repetition when implementing the S-M-I-L-E-S method of interacting with your children. You have to practice until it becomes second nature and you too can bounce back when you stumble. It's not easy, but it will work. Just do it!

> *"The only place success comes before work is in the dictionary."* **—Vince Lombardi**[137]

This is the attitude you must have about being a father and a husband. It's your attitude that sets the tone for your family. If you are constantly questioning your performance, you will convey this attitude to your children. Confidence is contagious. **Support** it in your children's lives. **Model** it for **Imitation**. Help them develop the self-discipline and **Limit**-setting ability to persevere, especially during tough times. **Educate** them about accepting failure as a process that ultimately leads to success. Most of all help them see that reliance on faith and **Spirituality** will help them overcome all the obstacles life puts before them.

> *"Implement the S-M-I-L-E-S program and you will be a gold-medal dad."* **—Dr. T**

INSTANT REPLAY

- Allow your child to try new things and do not look at failure as the final result.
- Help your child understand that adversity is to be cherished.

- See trying and failing as a process—learning to overcome adversity.
- Model the courage to attack failures—changing a negative into a positive.
- Develop a positive attitude to inspire people around you.
- Take responsibility for your actions and don't blame others.
- Train yourself to have a confident outlook and never question your ability.
- Practice, practice, practice.
- Learn to laugh and have fun. Be a kid. Enjoy life.

"I always thought I could do whatever was necessary to succeed." **—Michael Jordan**[138]

CHAPTER 11

RESILIENCE

Adjusting to Misfortune and Change

"There will be times when you stumble and fall. However, if your fundamentals are in place, they will act as a safety net. You will always bounce back up." —**Lou Holtz**[139]

According to the dictionary, *resilience* is defined as "an ability to recover from or adjust easily to misfortune or change." It is a critical concept to understand when it comes to parenting.

Resilience is the ability to withstand whatever the world throws at us. We all want our kids to be able to bounce back, to hang in there when adversity shows itself. There are, however, critical circumstances we must consider when we apply the concept to raising kids.

Kids are developing, growing organisms coping with psychological, biological, and social stressors as they mature through childhood and adolescence. If the stressors are overwhelming, children fail to develop normally. They become mired in maladaptive behaviors, leading to failure and despair. If they're not challenged enough, they never develop the internal strength to respond to life's inevitable hardships. Raising resilient kids then becomes a balance of support and challenge: supporting protectively to foster development and providing challenges to ensure the capacity to overcome adversity.

Here is what the leading researchers say about resilience. Some see it as being resourceful, having the ability to solve problems, to bounce back, and to learn from mistakes. Resilience can be seen as a type of intelligence, which allows a person to learn from experience, fit into the environment, and think through problems in novel ways. We all know people who have "street sense" that allows them to adapt and survive but who can't do well in academic or more conventional pursuits.

Two researchers, Arnold Sameroff and Katherine Rosenblum, have studied resilience in children for a generation. They identified a group of children and tried to determine what factors influenced their development. They knew that certain risk factors could be associated with poor outcomes for kids. They hoped to identify one or two that were more likely to cause problems for the children as they matured.

The researchers followed these children and their families for thirty years, from infancy through adulthood. They looked at parenting attitudes, mental illnesses, and levels of education. Having a single parent, a large family, and stressful events were other risk factors.

The results were surprising, with individual risk factors not as important as the total number of stressors to which the children were exposed. Those children from families with no environmental risks scored thirty points higher on intelligence testing than those with eight to nine risk factors.

None of the children in the zero-risk group had an IQ below 85 (average IQ is 100), whereas almost 30 percent in the high-risk group scored below 85. The children's IQs dropped by an average of four points for every risk factor they encountered in their lives. Those who had five or more risk factors were 12.3 times as likely to have clinically meaningful mental health symptoms. For one group to be twice as likely to have mental health problems would be highly significant, but to be 12.3 times more likely is truly astounding.

Sameroff and Rosenblum reassessed the children several times throughout the thirty-year follow-up. The results remained consistent. Highly stressed families continued to have the same risk factors. They were unable to change their environments. Even if the children had been felt to be resilient as infants, they were pulled down by the high-risk environments. Highly competent children in high-risk families did worse than less competent kids in low-stress situations. Their school performance suffered, and their mental health deteriorated. Even at age thirty, those who had been identified as "resilient" as four-year-olds did not do well if they came from high-risk families.

Certainly the at-risk children were raised in less-than-ideal circumstances, but the findings are scary. As parents, we need to be aware of our actions and our circumstances if we're to raise competent and intelligent children. The researchers were quick to point out, "The majority of children in every social class and ethnic group are not failures. They get jobs; they have successful social relationships, and raise a new generation of children."

> *"Life is not a matter of holding good cards but of playing a poor hand well."* **—Robert Louis Stevenson, writer (1850–1894)**[140]

After completing a twenty-year study of competence and resilience in 205 children, 27 percent of whom were minorities, psychologist Ann Masten found that the minority children who were able to succeed in spite of adversity had more internal and external resources. They especially had good thinking skills and were exposed to effective parenting. The resilient minority children were much like competent children with less stress in their lives. They could solve problems, were able to learn and pay attention, and could follow rules and the laws of society. The adults in their lives provided age-appropriate structure, high expectations for performance, and a warm, caring environment.

The children who did not do well had few protective resources. They were overwhelmed by adversity without the support of close relationships with competent adults. The at-risk kids developed significant problems as adolescents. They were inclined to be stressed and were more likely to have difficulty coping. Their self-esteem was quite low, and they struggled to make it in life.

The researchers located the children in the study for the twenty-year follow-up. As the young adults developed romantic relationships and began to work, it became clear that success was related to earlier competence. They found that some of the less competent young people in this study were able to turn their lives around. It seemed that breaking ties with negative peer groups, marrying the right person, and serving in the military helped some of the troubled youth take a different path.

Some of the children had become homeless, but even these children were able to demonstrate high academic achievement if their parents were there for them. Those children whose parents were involved in their education, communicated high expectations for success, and insured school attendance and the completion of homework did well. Supportive parents produce competent children even in the most adverse situations.

Here is a short list of protective factors suggested by the research.

- First on the list was having "ordinary parents." As a parent, you don't have to be exceptional. You don't have to be perfect—average will do—but you do have to be there. It's called *support*!
- Having "connections to other competent and caring adults" came second. Children need adults in their lives in order to succeed.
- Those who had "intelligence and good intellectual skills" fared better.
- Resilient kids had a "sense of self-efficacy." In other words, they felt in control of their lives and felt that they were capable of performing well.
- Resilient kids were "appealing to others." They were able to make a connection, and this may reflect their capacity to establish meaningful positive relationships.
- These kids developed talents that were valued by themselves and those around them. They had a sense of "meaning in life."
- Resilient kids had "faith and developed religious connections."
- "Coming from higher socioeconomic groups, attending good schools, and having community resources available" helped out but were not essential.[141]

Other research has looked at the mechanisms of resilience from biological and psychological perspectives. One study focused on individuals who were exposed to extreme stress and yet showed remarkable resilience.

Extensive interviews were conducted with a group of 750 men, mostly pilots, many of whom were in captivity during the Vietnam War. A number of them were held in Vietnamese prisons for six to eight years, tortured, and kept in solitary confinement.

These individuals were thoroughly evaluated through "videotaped interviews, neuropsychological testing (including tests of emotional intelligence), neuro-imaging, and DNA studies." Every attempt was made to learn as much as possible about how they were able to survive physically, intellectually, and emotionally.

As a result of this research, ten critical elements of resilience were identified.[142]

1. *Optimism.*

In my mind, optimism is so important to instill in our children that I devoted a whole chapter to the issue of failure and a positive attitude. A positive attitude should pervade your home. When you leave for work every morning, you should tell your family to have a great day. You need to talk optimistically about your work and your recreational activities.

Find something positive to say to each family member every day. This does not mean you have to ignore the realities of life, but it does mean that you and your spouse should interact in a positive way with your children. By helping them look on the bright side of difficult situations, you will allow them to expand their horizons and not fear failure.

Optimism is powerful. It saved the lives of many of the 750 men who endured torture, separation from loved ones, and horrible living conditions. Helping your children become optimistic about life will pay dividends down the line. It will instill in them the "can-do attitude," which will carry them forward on the job, in their homes, and in their communities.

Optimism helps our children find meaning in adversity. This creates a positive acceptance of difficulties in life and allows the development of a sense of competence. "Hang in there; you can do it. Just break it down into small steps and go at them one at a time. We can beat this problem; it'll just take some time."

Part of being positive has to do with being able to think flexibly. Research has shown that resilient individuals can reframe challenging situations in a more positive light. It's like the old saying "look on the bright side." Flexibility of thought allows the resilient person to see a problem as being only temporary and manageable. Negative, inflexible individuals often will interpret their problems as being interminable and overwhelming.

Encouraging flexible thinking will provide your children with the ability to change what they can and to accept what they cannot change. You do not reflect flexibility of thinking if you're up against a brick wall pounding your head on it in hopes of knocking it over. You might want to look for a way to get around it or over it. You can still maintain a positive attitude and certainly avoid a headache.

2. Altruism.

Parents can demonstrate their commitment to altruistic endeavors and set the example of giving of themselves in various ways—volunteering for community organizations and giving time or money to charities.

Adopting a less fortunate family to help in times of need can be a family project. We often think about helping others during the holiday seasons, but poverty and misery are year-round conditions for many. Volunteering at a homeless shelter or making visits to an old folks' home can be extremely rewarding. Involving children can give them a sense of compassion and help them learn firsthand what it feels like to be of assistance to others.

I can speak from personal experience. While attending Stanford University, I worked on a fraternity community service project at a school for the developmentally disabled, a project that resulted in my becoming a child and adolescent psychiatrist. As a physician, I know how gratifying it can be to help another human being. I am blessed to be in a profession that allows me to help others on a daily basis. It just makes for a good feeling inside.

Participation is the key to ingraining altruism into the characters of our children. Money and gifts are fine, but actively helping someone is a better learning experience. You never know; it may be a life-changing event.

3. *Having a moral compass.*

Having a set of beliefs that cannot be destroyed made a huge difference for the prisoners of war in Vietnam. Unshakable standards provide a bulwark against moral compromise that ultimately can lead to moral decay. Helping our children understand the importance of doing right and avoiding wrong is crucial to helping them become functioning adults. If they develop a set of morals for their behavior, they will gain the respect of those around them and solidify the self-respect within. Knowing that you are doing right goes a long way toward getting the job done. It provides an inner strength and resilience beyond measure.

4. *Faith and spirituality.*

These qualities were very important attributes found in resilient survivors. Faith and spirituality are so important that I have devoted a chapter to spirituality in this book. It addresses the importance that coaches place on spirituality and the benefits of religious participation.

5. *Humor.*

Resilient individuals have been found to appreciate humor and use it regularly in their lives. The experts categorize humor as a "mature defense mechanism."[143] I guess that means if you can laugh when the computer shuts down and you lose three pages of your best work, you have just illustrated the concept of a mature defense mechanism. The irony of the computer glitch occurring while writing this chapter commands that I model mature behavior for the readers and laugh it off rather than become infuriated, yell @$#%^&*, and quit writing for the day.

Humor is a great coping strategy and has been shown to decrease the risk of stress-induced depression. Studies of resilient Vietnam veterans, cancer patients, at-risk children, and surgical patients demonstrate the use of humor as a healthy, active coping mechanism. Humor allows us to defuse the tension and reassess the situation more realistically. Humor puts a positive light on the problem and allows us to confront adversity from a more positive perspective. Mothers whose children were undergoing bone marrow transplants (a very painful procedure) were less depressed if they could use humor to deal with the situation.

Having a sense of humor makes it less likely for a person to become depressed. It's hard to be depressed if you can laugh at the situation. Humor is fun. That's why we have comics and the ancient kings had court jesters. We pay good money to have people make us laugh. Laughter should be part of everyday life in the family. It helps establish social bonds and enables our children to develop important relationships in life.

We don't have to teach our kids to be the life of the party, but we do need to help them see the humorous side of life. A joke a day keeps the drug dealer away. Resilient, happy kids have no use for drugs. Drugs and alcohol stimulate the same part of the brain that is activated when we laugh. No joke!

The ability to laugh at ourselves is an essential part of self-assessment and critical to the establishment of an excellent role model for our kids.

6. *Having an appropriate role model.*

A role model is someone to look up to and to serve as a guide for behavior and attitude. This can make all the difference for a child. If we set the example, our children will then choose other role models more appropriately. If we tell them not to do something and then do it ourselves, how can we expect them to do it differently?

If you want your children to choose a drug dealer as a role model, keep smoking pot. If you want them to aspire to something greater, you have to model it through diligence and hard work. Modeling is addressed more completely in an earlier chapter.

7. *An ability to establish social supports.*

Social support has been found to reduce stress and improve both emotional and physical well-being. A study of people in Alameda County, California, found that men and women without social supports were much more likely to die from cancer, stroke, and other illnesses.[144] Not having an extensive social support system appeared to be as much of a negative to health as high blood pressure, obesity, cigarette smoking, and a lack of physical activity.

Good social support reduces the chance of developing depression, and if depression does occur, it makes relapse less likely. Even if someone is predisposed to depression, having a good social network will reduce the likelihood of depression occurring.

The risk of developing post-traumatic stress disorder (PTSD) was significantly reduced by the presence of a good social support system.[145] Social support and religious involvement can have a significant positive effect on anyone's life. Helping our children understand the importance of developing relationships and friendships will go a long way toward assisting them in becoming resilient adults. "Plays well with others" is a comment we want to see on our children's report cards. Highly successful individuals have a common attribute: good people skills. It really is more fun if you do things with people, and it's healthier too.

8. *The ability to face fears.*

Facing our fears is another active coping mechanism that enables us to make use of fear in an appropriate manner. Those who tell you they have never been afraid are lying or dead. It is good to be fearful in dangerous situations. Fear is built into our biological makeup for survival reasons. You can only walk along the edge of a cliff so long before you make a misstep. Teasing the grizzly bear one too many times can be fatal.

Resilient individuals use fear as a warning sign. A heightened awareness that comes with fear allows us to evaluate a threat more accurately and to initiate an appropriate response. Resilient individuals can face both internal and external fears and overcome them, but often a fear of failure makes it difficult to progress.

I know from my experience as a child and adolescent psychiatrist that children and adults who are traumatized by physical and sexual abuse must face their memories head-on in order to recover. Reducing the emotional impact of those horrific memories through repetition in a safe environment is the toughest thing they may ever do in their lives. It is, however, a testimony to their resilience.

9. *Having a mission in life.*

It is important to have a mission in life in order to give life meaning. Resilient individuals set goals for themselves in life and go about accomplishing them. Helping our children set immediate and long-term goals will assist them in becoming successful. It's about having a game plan. It's like opening savings accounts for our children's tuitions to college on the day they are born. We have a goal of seeing that our children obtain quality educations in order to be afforded the best chances of success.

We help them understand as they progress through their schooling that good grades now mean more opportunities and options later in life. Assignments and tests are hurdles that need to be cleared on the way to the finish line. One accomplishment builds on another and advances them toward the goal of excellence in whatever field they choose to pursue.

10. *Training.*

Yes, you can train to be resilient. Being physically active is an important part of self-care, because it has a positive effect on mood, physical fitness, and self-esteem. Exercise relieves stress, helps deal with negative emotions, and is part of an active coping style. Exercise causes our brains to produce growth factors (brain-derived neurotropic factor, or BDNF) that enhance the connectivity between brain cells. A brain stimulated by physical activity operates more efficiently and effectively.

A study of older men and women between the ages of sixty-five and ninety-two demonstrated improved intellectual functioning for those who exercised regularly.[146]

Training our bodies also trains our minds. A disciplined approach to physical training serves as a template for a disciplined approach to life. Helping children push their boundaries—physically, emotionally, and intellectually—ensures resiliency. Every task they complete, every hurdle they surmount, every mountain they climb gives them confidence to move forward in life.

Long-term studies consistently illustrate the critical nature of early life experiences for our children. The environment we provide as parents will have

RESILIENCE

an indelible impact on our children and grandchildren. The attributes we can cultivate in our children to enhance their capacity to adapt and succeed bear repeating.

INSTANT REPLAY

- Maintain an optimistic outlook and instill it in your children.
- Demonstrate your commitment to charity and helping others.
- Help your children understand the importance of doing right and avoiding wrong.
- Teach the importance of faith and spirituality.
- Appreciate humor and use it regularly.
- Provide good role models for your children to imitate.
- Help them develop social supports to reduce stress and improve emotional and physical well-being.
- Assist children in learning to face their fears.
- Help set goals for their lives and assist them in accomplishing those goals.
- Train children to push their physical, emotional, and intellectual boundaries to ensure resilience.

> *"If you want to see a great fighter at his best, watch him when he is getting beat." —**Sugar Ray Robinson**,[147] greatest welterweight and middleweight boxer of the twentieth century*

> *"The greatest accomplishment is not in never falling but in rising again after you fall." —**Vince Lombardi**[148]*

CHAPTER 12

PARENTING AS A TEAM

The Game Plan

"The most important measure of how good a game I had played was how much better I had made my teammates play." —Bill Russell, Boston Celtics, Naismith Memorial Basketball Hall of Famer[149]

Former National Basketball Association head coach Pat Riley has stated, "Family life is the central team experience." Central to family life is caring. Coaches in all sports emphasize the importance of caring about team members. It is essential to the development of team spirit and cohesion.

The depth of caring in a family is exemplified best by the story of one survivor of the "miracle on the Hudson" plane crash near New York City. When told the plane was going down, he hurriedly scratched a message to his family on a business card. He wrote how much he loved them and placed it in his pocket. Assuming the crash position, he awaited his fate. This hero understood his family's need for comfort should he die. He was demonstrating empathy, an essential human attribute.

To understand any situation someone might be experiencing, we have to put ourselves in his or her shoes—have empathy. Empathy is a characteristic that even the toughest, most competitive athletes display. It is the quality of understanding the feelings of others, but it has many forms that correspond to emotions, which are being observed, like fear, pain, or joy.

To illustrate the point, let me give you an example of how empathy pertains to sports. In an FSN show called *Sports Science*, a group of professional athletes was shown films of some memorable sports events—memorable because of the horrendous injuries that occurred during them. They were shown a hockey goalie having his neck sliced open by a skate, a pitcher taking a line drive to his face, and a player getting hit in the testicles by a tennis ball, among others. While viewing the games, the athletes' respiration and pulse rates were measured.

Many of the professional athletes showed their emotions directly by grimacing, cringing, and swearing. The experiences also registered in their brains because their breathing rates increased by 25 percent, and their pulse rates increased by 70 percent. The empathy that the athletes showed was real and had both emotional and physical impacts on them.

You might wonder why human beings would have empathy programmed into their brains. Women are certainly more empathetic when it comes to emotions. When they see and hear a crying child, they immediately rush to its side. Women typically cry with a person who is sad and provide physical support through hugging and touching.

This behavior may have survival implications for the species. Rescuing children in distress certainly increases the likelihood that they will live into adulthood. Establishing social bonds with other women ensures the likelihood that someone will be available for support in times of difficulty. This is the "tend and befriend" response.

For guys, it's a team thing. When hunting woolly mammoths with a sharp rock on a stick, the team in pursuit needs to function at the highest level. Success would not take place unless the hunters could work together in a coordinated fashion. If a member were hurt, it would affect the whole group, not just the individual. If every injured individual were just left to die, a team would soon be depleted. For survival's sake, recognizing that another person is experiencing pain and might be injured is a very important human attribute.

This is the appeal of team sports for fans. Fans can experience all the emotions of the players and coaches vicariously. Humans enjoy sharing emotions. Why else would they pack themselves into one-hundred-thousand-seat stadiums, endure traffic jams, and pay outrageous prices to view a sporting event?

PARENTING AS A TEAM

Why do we have friends over to watch the Masters Golf Tournament, the Stanley Cup, the Super Bowl, and the Final Four? It's all about sharing emotion—"the thrill of victory and the agony of defeat." This is why guys want to share sports and outdoor experiences with their children and families. They want to experience the emotions associated with catching that first fish or organizing and carrying out the hunt. When guys take their children to their first baseball game, it reminds them of their own experiences with their fathers.

We all have a sense of accomplishment and joy when our favorite college team sinks a three-pointer at the buzzer. We have that same anticipation as the players on the sideline when the quarterback throws into the end zone with five seconds left on the clock. At a football game, we become one with the players, coaches, and all of those around us screaming, jumping up and down, and bursting with joy when the ball is caught for a touchdown. We hug people we don't know; we slap them on the back and treat them as if they were lifelong friends.

This illustrates the importance of establishing a team approach to parenting. There are actually mirror neurons in our brains that turn on when we see something happen to someone else. These neurons make us feel like we're experiencing the event ourselves. The statement "I feel your pain" is accurate from our brains' perspective.

Benjamin Franklin, when discussing the implications of signing the Declaration of Independence, said, "We must all hang together or we shall most assuredly all hang separately." This could not be truer when applied to parenting. We've got one shot at raising a child, and if we don't act as a team, we will go down in defeat. The question is: How do we develop a cohesive team to take on this daunting task?

We must remember that a team is made up of individuals with different strengths and weaknesses. We've already discussed how men and women are different. Women are certainly better at dealing with emotions. In fact, guys, we're just outclassed. That does not mean that we get off the hook. Even though we're not naturals in this area, we are trainable. It all gets back to repetition, repetition, repetition, and more repetition. Women may have greater difficulty in being disciplinarians, but they can learn to set limits effectively.

As part of developing a parenting team, you need to assess the team's positive and negative attributes. This means doing an accurate self-assessment, making the necessary lists, and looking back at the parenting skills of our parents and grandparents. Where did one set of parents shine and the other falter? You can pick out the best parts of those styles and incorporate them into your own team approach to parenting—your playbook.

If you've got a big game coming up, you would not just review one film of your opponent; you'd find as many as you could. The same is true of parenting. You have to dig a little, look back over your own lives, and pick out the trends before you can develop your game plan.

We learn about the concept of a team very early in life. We may not label the parenting couple as a team, but it is the basis for raising a child. There are some who would say fathers are not essential to a child's development. They would point to the fact that many children are raised by single mothers at times with very good outcomes. The overwhelming majority of folks, both professionals and laypeople, would disagree. Dads are important and should not be relegated to sitting on the bench, while moms do most of the work.

As fathers, being part of a team, we must consider the needs and concerns of our spouses. Unfortunately, we live in the "me generation." Many feel they deserve everything in life and that their needs are the only ones that count. It does not work that way on a team or in a marriage. As a team, we have to look out for each other, be aware of the feelings of others, and in some situations, place our needs below those of our spouses.

We should wake up every morning, thinking, *What can I do today to make life easier for the mother of my children? What will help her do her job better?* Let's face it. Women do most of the heavy lifting when it comes to taking care of the family. We might bring in a paycheck that puts food on the table, but our responsibility does not end there. This is especially true when those we often characterize as being our better halves are also working outside the home.

We need to understand the stresses women experience as they try to balance responsibilities. Asking them how they are feeling and listening to their frustrations will go a long way toward helping them feel supported and cared for. Even if it means missing fifteen minutes of *Monday Night Football*, we can do it because we're "gold-medal" dads.

Many times, our choice of a spouse will determine the type of parental team we will have. Did we pick a spouse who holds the same values, has similar views on parenting, and came from a similar background?

Developing a parenting team is not unlike raising a child. The same S-M-I-L-E-S concept applies. Couples must:

- Support each other in order to survive;
- Model the behavior for their spouse to
- Imitate (in other words, treat your spouse as you would like to be treated);
- Limit-set for themselves as well as for the children;
- Educate and teach each other (through daily communication); and
- Spiritually be bonded, which will enhance all other aspects of parenting.

Support

Well, how does this work in real life? How can a guy implement the process? What is the most appropriate way to demonstrate support? Let me count the ways! Helping out around the house does a lot to reduce stress for your spouse.

A study out of the University of California looked at stress levels and satisfaction with marriage.[150] The researchers found a difference between men and women. The level of stress hormones measured in women was much less if they were satisfied in their relationship and marriage. This correlated with their spouses helping with the kids, meals, and general household chores. The men's stress hormones were related to how busy they were at work rather than how they viewed their home life.

Stress levels affect relationships, and parental relationships affect parenting. It's important to ask your spouse, "What can I do to help?" It sounds simple, but it can give your harried spouse a feeling of support. The important thing is being there, being fully present. Knowing someone cares enough about you to offer assistance can make a huge difference.

Modeling for Imitation

Treating each other with respect not only models good interactions for the kids but sets up the expectation for both parents to treat each other as they would like to be treated. If a parent is striving to be the best spouse possible and modeling appropriate parenting behaviors, it's bound to rub off on the spouse and the children.

Teach each other by example, not by word. When we demonstrate a caring, loving relationship toward one another, those behaviors and interactions are incorporated by others around us. It's like magic. Positive behaviors and statements produce positive statements and behaviors, creating a cascade of good feelings. This makes it easy to copy and incorporate those actions that make us feel good about ourselves.

Limits

We all have limits. When operating as a team, it is extremely important to establish limits for ourselves both individually and collectively. In order to reduce conflict and stress, it is essential to delineate the limits of our capabilities. All too often, we try to take on too much and become overextended and stressed. We fail to accomplish our goals and ultimately blame someone else for our failure. This can result in frustration and bickering.

Sitting down with your spouse and prioritizing your goals can go a long way toward preventing a cycle of unrealistic expectations, unfulfilled accomplishments, anger, and resentment. It may be necessary at times to tell your spouse you can't do something. You may not want to do it, and that's okay. You may not have time to do it or feel that there are other priorities requiring your attention. It's okay to say no. You must understand, however, that your spouse has the same rights.

Education

Much is made of communication in marriage and rightly so. As parents, educating each other about the family interactions is essential to a well-functioning team. Discussing parenting issues with your spouse on a daily basis sets up a proactive forum for preventing problems. It gives both parents a chance to give their viewpoints on family issues and hear different perspectives. A unified approach can be developed for interactions with children and a game plan developed to deal with problem issues.

Communication is crucial for dealing with the daily trials of raising kids. It prevents manipulation on their part and cements a sense of teamwork between the adults. It's just like on the playing field. You need to let the quarterback know you can get open on a certain route if you expect to get the ball.

Spirituality

Marriage is a spiritual bond for the purpose of raising children. It means a long-lasting commitment to each other and also to the family. Spirituality in the family may manifest itself in various forms. Certainly, moral standards incorporating not only the don'ts but the dos in life should be part of the family structure. Honesty, integrity, and awareness of the rights of others are moral constructs that can be viewed as spiritual in nature and contribute to the bond between the parenting team.

Praying, attending religious services, and participating in religiously oriented activities all contribute to the spiritual component of family life. Having a mutual moral compass and a set of unshakable beliefs contributes not only to the resilience of the marriage but resilience in the children as well. Establishing a tradition of giving to others who may be less fortunate should be an important tenet of family life. Altruism benefits the giver much more than the receiver and as we have learned contributes to resilience.

The Game Plan

Yogi Berra, the New York Yankee player and coach, emphasized the need for a game plan when he said, "If you don't know where you're going, you will wind up somewhere else." He added a hint of caution with his admonishment, "You've got to be very careful if you don't know where you're going because you might not get there." It's very easy to go off in several directions if you don't take the time to develop a comprehensive approach to parenting. You don't want to place yourself in a position that Yogi found himself in, when the person he was riding with said, "I think we're lost." Yogi responded, "Yeah, but we're making good time."

It does no good to go barreling ahead if you're headed in the wrong direction. It just takes you further off course and away from the goal of developing a cohesive, consistent plan for raising your kids. Many times, parents want to "play it by ear," wing it, improvise as they go along, and hope for the best. Planning takes time and effort up front but can make a world of difference in the long run.

*"It's like déjà vu all over again." —**Yogi Berra**[151]*

Yogi was right. We parent like we were parented. Your interactions with your children repeat your parents' interactions with you. This makes it really tough because you have ingrained patterns of parenting that your folks modeled for you. How can you change those modeled and ingrained parenting behavior patterns, which may not have been effective or appropriate?

PARENTING AS A TEAM

You have to sit down with your spouse at the very beginning of your parenting experience and decide how you plan to handle various situations as parents. And as the kids get older, you may want to include them in the problem-solving process. A better way to put it may be "problem-preventing" process. The three Ps are problem, preventing, and process. The problem-preventing-process concept is crucial to being a great dad. "An ounce of prevention is worth a pound of cure." You are the hero if you can predict the problem before it occurs and prevent it from happening.

If you remember the three Ps—problem, preventing, and process—you will go a long way toward making your life and the lives of those around you more pleasant and productive.

Some real-life examples of using the three Ps might be illustrated best by the following scenarios.

- *Problem*: Your toddler has a habit of pulling things down on the floor when going from one thing to the next around the room.
- *Prevention*: You can save yourself considerable aggravation by putting things up out of reach.
- *Process*: Sounds simple, but it may mean getting up out of your easy chair the minute your child enters the room. It is a minor inconvenience but a great preventive intervention.

- *Problem*: Your ten-year-old frequently sneaks off to play video games without your knowledge. When you catch him, it typically results in a big blowup.
- *Prevention*: The video game controller becomes your property, and your child has to check it out.
- *Process*: There still may be some argument, but it's much less of a hassle than it would have been. Try to anticipate the problem before it occurs. Discuss potential interventions with your spouse and simplify your life.

Many decisions that we have to make as parents need not be made immediately. This is the hard part. When do you wait and watch, and when do you act decisively and immediately? Many times, you have to go back to the basics. *What can I do to be supportive? How can I be a good role model in this situation? Do I need to set limits and how forcefully? How can I make this an educational experience? What higher moral concept do I need to impart, if any?*

If we are going to respond immediately in a situation, we have to have the basics down. And it's back to pitching and catching, dribbling and passing, blocking and tackling, running and kicking. The fundamentals need to be established and become automatic. Yogi once said, "Think? How the hell are you going to think and hit at the same time?"

Parenting over time can become almost instinctive and automatic, but you still have to think. You still have to go back to the game plan. You have to analyze the situation and sometimes call *an audible*. You can use visualization to project an outcome. You have to think beyond the immediate, avoid the distraction, and throw the ball to where the receiver is going to be without hesitation. The same holds true in parenting. If you plan ahead, if you practice, the outcome won't always be perfect, but you will master the situation more often than not.

When we talk about a game plan, it should not be viewed as something set in stone. Just like a coach at halftime will reassess what the team has accomplished or not accomplished during the first half, parents need to adjust their approach frequently. Parents have the problem of dealing with a developing and hopefully maturing child with ever-changing needs. Parents must be adaptable in order to survive.

We might get headed in the right direction with everything going well and then find out we took a wrong turn. Sometimes it's good to retrace your steps, reset your compass, consult the operating manual, review the playbook, and maybe even change the game plan.

An aphorism that comes to mind is "look before you leap." We don't always have to *do something* as parents. Sometimes it's more important to wait and watch rather than act immediately. Many times, parents feel on the spot. They are told by experts that they should intervene immediately in order to have maximum effect on their child's behavior. This is true if a toddler is about to pull over a pot of boiling water or if a teenager announces he or she is going to start smoking pot—a swift "No" should follow. It wouldn't be bad to add "over my dead body" for a little emphasis. In some situations, however, waiting, watching, and analyzing may produce a better outcome.

When implementing a game plan, it is important to keep things as simple as possible. Most parenting books will emphasize understanding the meaning of certain behaviors and feeling states when interacting with children: *you must be careful not to bruise their developing sense of self-esteem when you interact with them.* It's as if helping them understand why it is important to take out the trash or wash the dishes will get the job done.

Unfortunately, psychiatry and psychology have placed too much emphasis on attempting to understand behavior. Children don't need to have their feelings considered every time they are asked to do something. The expectation should be that they will do it. They don't need to like it; they don't need to understand it; they don't need to express their feelings about it; they just need to do it.

A perfect example of this approach to child rearing is a foster-parent couple who have taken more than sixty children into their home over a period of thirteen years. The Burtons live in a 2,500-square-foot home in Kuna, Idaho. Their story appeared in the October 23, 2006, edition of the *Idaho Statesman*.

The Burtons specialize in taking the most difficult cases from the Idaho Department of Health and Welfare. The neglected children have been physically, emotionally, or sexually abused, and 80 percent of their parents have severe drug or alcohol problems.

Foster mom Kandra Burton was quoted as saying, "Unspeakable things have happened to these kids." All the children have severe behavioral problems. The Burtons make it plain to the children that they will only be their parents for a short time. Mrs. Burton went on to say, "I tell them that I am their temporary mom, and it's my job to find them a real mom and dad and teach them the skills to make it work."

The Burtons have a very simple approach to child rearing. They emphasize routine and consistent behavior. This is new to many of the children who have never experienced consistency in the chaotic and erratic lives they have led before placement. Many have been homeless—living with drug-addicted, unpredictable, unstructured parents.

The Burtons' rules are simple and straightforward. Everyone goes to school or work every day. Everyone washes their hands, brushes their teeth, and combs their hair. Everyone sits down at the table and eats dinner. Evenings are spent reading or watching a movie. "The kids need someone to count on," Burton said, "someone to pick them up from school, and someone to fix dinner."

Life at the Burtons' is not extravagant; it's just normal. Everyone is expected to follow the house rules, do their chores, and participate in family activities. Going to the store and planning a meal is the Burtons' idea of an adventure. There are no special privileges; everyone gets treated the same.

Kandra Burton does not want to know details of the children's former lives. She feels that this in some way may cause her to feel sorry for her charges and bend the rules. She knows that this would be wrong and would compromise her effectiveness as a parent. Rules are rules, and expectations need to be met on a daily basis.

Mrs. Burton remembers a nine-year-old boy who prior to being placed in her home had spent his whole life living in a car. The boy had not spent any time playing with other children and had never attended school. His hair had been allowed to grow until it reached his hips. He had never had a haircut in his life. The routine in the home was that everyone received a haircut before starting school. This boy was no exception. It was surely a frightening experience for him, but he survived and thrived.

The Burtons created an environment of emotional and physical support. They modeled appropriate and caring behaviors for imitation and set firm, appropriate limits for the youngsters. They emphasized the importance of school and learning and, by their behavior, modeled the importance of altruism and moral commitment. It sounds an awful lot like the S-M-I-L-E-S program.

Consistency

As mentioned before, game plans should not be static but dynamic. Sometimes we undertake a course of action in the parenting process and feel like we can't change. If we do, we will be labeled inconsistent. In politics, we hear how candidates "flip-flop" on issues. It's like there's something wrong with you if you find out that the plan is not working and you change course.

> *"A foolish consistency is the hobgoblin of small minds."*—**Ralph Waldo Emerson**[152]

The ability to change direction is an essential skill for parenting as well as for life. As John Wooden said, "Change is inevitable, and failure to change at the appropriate time may be catastrophic."

The CEO, the plant manager, the foreman, and the individual worker sometimes make the mistake of maintaining consistency no matter what. The CEO says, "We've been doing it this way for the last ten years; why change now?" (It hasn't worked yet.) The company manager hasn't controlled costs, and the plant produces shoddy products. The foreman is despised by his men, and the line worker continues to do things the same way over and over and over because it would be a pain to even think about change. Everything goes down the tubes; the company goes bankrupt; and the employees lose their jobs. They all feel like they are failures, but, boy, were they consistent! (Of course they could always ask for a government bailout—an option not available to most parents.)

You have to constantly reevaluate what you're doing and how you're doing it on a daily basis. I wish there were an easier way, but parenting is a job that is in constant flux. It's a challenge, but that is what life is all about.

I would not want you to think that you should banish *consistency* from your parenting vocabulary. Being consistent in the enforcement of rules and responsibilities is part of the structural support families provide for children.

Inconsistent rule enforcement makes riverboat gamblers out of your kids. A multibillion-dollar industry is based on the principle of intermittent reinforcement. This is the psychological concept behind slot machines, black jack, roulette, and many more gaming-industry methods for separating us from our hard-earned cash.

Intermittent reinforcement means that the "house" lets you win from time to time in order to give you the expectation of bigger returns on the next pull of the handle, turn of the card, or bounce of the ball. When parents are inconsistent in rule enforcement, kids will start to gamble that Mom or Dad is going to give in this time. This actually causes them to be more persistent in their attempts to catch the folks napping or changing their minds.

You may find that your child has been successful in manipulating you. You are now determined to change your behavior and be more consistent with the rules. Watch out! When you start enforcing a rule and giving the child consequences for negative behavior, the negative behavior will increase for a period of time. They will test you to see if you are really going to follow through consistently. Any behavior will require at least one month to see change. It won't happen overnight. This goes for other types of behavior such as exercise and diet.

If children do not respond in thirty days and continue the negative behavior, they may be seeking negative attention. Yes, kids do get all the attention they need, and acting out in negative ways is one way to get it. If this is happening, continue reading the next chapter.

Above all, as a parent, you need to follow the advice of Woody Hayes, the great Ohio State football coach: "Be a pragmatist. First find out what works. Then keep on doing it."[153]

INSTANT REPLAY

- Support each other in order to survive;
- Model the behavior for your spouse to
- Imitate (in other words, treat your spouse as you would like to be treated);
- Limits need to be set for yourselves as well as for the children;

PARENTING AS A TEAM

- Educate and teach each other (through daily communication); and
- Spiritually and morally bond with each other to enhance all other aspects of parenting.

> *"All that I accomplished is not because of me. It is because of God and my offensive line."* **—Walter Payton, running back, Pro Football Hall of Famer**[154]

FOURTH QUARTER

"Having a child is surely the most beautiful, irrational act that two people in love can commit."
—**Bill Cosby, comedian**[155]

"Marriage is nature's way of keeping us from fighting with strangers." —**Alan King, comedian**[156]

"Marriage has no guarantees. If that's what you're looking for, go live with a car battery."
—**Erma Bombeck, author**[157]

CHAPTER 13

WHEN NOTHING WORKS

Troubleshooting Parenting Practices

"Face your deficiencies and acknowledge them. But do not let them master you." —**Helen Keller, American author rendered blind and deaf in childhood**[158]

It's important to understand some sobering statistics when it comes to problems your children may encounter in their lives.[159] The likelihood of developing a diagnosable psychiatric condition during life is quite high—46.4 percent. Half of all lifetime psychiatric problems will have their onset by the age of fourteen, and 75 percent will start by the age of twenty-four.

This means that many families will have children who experience a psychiatric problem before they finish college. Half of all cases of anxiety and impulse-control disorders will start before eleven years of age. Fifty percent of all substance use disorders will have their onset before the age of twenty. Mood disorders for many people occur later in life, but half of the people who develop them will do so by thirty years of age. This chapter will provide you with the information you need in order to address these issues for your child should they arise.

Parents are also at risk for developing a psychiatric condition. They have the same risk, almost 50 percent, of having a mental health problem as their children. While the statistics are sobering, early recognition and treatment can allow both parents and children to live normal, productive lives.

Having a mental health condition is no longer the problem it once was. The stigma is less, and more treatments are available. Unfortunately, not recognizing the problem and not obtaining early treatment can lead to deadly results.

The suicide rate for untreated bipolar disorder has been estimated as being between 15 and 25 percent. The unfortunate reality is that bipolar disorder is under-recognized and under-treated. On average, it is ten years from the onset of bipolar symptoms until it is diagnosed correctly. Most individuals with this condition will see three clinicians before appropriate treatment is initiated.

Recent statistics for adolescents showed the leading cause of death was accidents, which accounted for 6,825 deaths in 2004. The second leading cause of death was homicides, which amounted to 1,932 premature deaths in the same year. Suicide was the third leading cause of death at 1,700. The homicide rate for blacks was almost six times that of the white population, whereas the Hispanic homicide rate was three times that of whites. Whites were twice as likely as blacks to kill themselves.

Many of these tragic occurrences could have been prevented had the underlying psychiatric condition been treated. We will see in a later chapter the importance of attending religious services in reducing these risks of unintentional accidents, suicides, and homicides. Resilient and competent children are much less likely to succumb to these devastating and preventable events.

When do these problems start for our kids? It has been estimated that 10 percent of young children in the United States experience a behavioral problem before the age of six. If the child is from an impoverished family, that number increases to 25 percent.

One study looked at 721 children over a period of eight years.[160] The researchers were attempting to understand the possible predictors of school-age behavior problems. The children in this study were by and large from middle-income families. Over half of the mothers in these families had attended some college, and 54 percent were two-income families with incomes well above the poverty line.

The researchers found that the temperament of the child was highly correlated with his or her behavioral difficulties. It is well known that difficult, temperamental children may not fit well in particular family settings. The parent-child interaction gets off track early in the child's life, and problems have a tendency to escalate over time.

Male children were more likely to have problems, and poor parenting ability significantly affected the probability of a positive outcome. The takeaway message from this study is to recognize the interactional difficulties early on and obtain help before serious problems develop.

> *"Knowing what is normal is one of the biggest challenges in parenting. 'Is my child different?'"*
> *—Dr. T*

Parenting is difficult. You didn't get a playbook. As parents, we don't want to think that our children can have a problem. *He's going to grow up to be a quarterback for the Dallas Cowboys or play guard for the Los Angeles Lakers. She won't have any difficulties; she'll get straight As in school, have lots of friends, and be rich beyond our wildest dreams. He'll marry a beautiful woman, and she'll marry a successful man, and they'll present us with lovely grandchildren to spoil.*

In actual fact, most of the time, our dreams are really just fantasies that are not related in any way to reality. Our kids will have problems, just like most parents' kids. The difficulty is that we didn't get a playbook to guide us.

It's normal to look the other way and deny trouble. It's only when we are confronted with the undeniable fact that someone outside the family—a teacher, the minister, a friend, hopefully not a police officer—has recognized our child has a problem that we may be able to look at it. Too often we doubt the source of the bad news, when we should be thankful that someone cared enough to tell us.

Acceptance of a problem is doubly hard for dads since they're often out of the loop when it comes to health-care and school decisions for their children. I know from experience; as a child and adolescent psychiatrist, I rarely see fathers who are directly involved in their child's treatment.

Dads many times are not involved until the family has gone through three babysitters or their child is failing in school. This lack of communication can be easily prevented if Mom and Dad talk on a daily basis about the children. Even then, because of the tendency to want things to go well, small issues can be ignored until a crisis brings them to the fore.

All parents are concerned about the development of their children. This starts at conception and goes through childhood and adolescence.

- Are they growing properly?
- Are they walking, talking, and completing toilet training on time?
- How are they progressing in school?
- Are they having difficulties learning or problems getting along with other children?
- How do they compare with kids who are the same age?
- Should they be involved in team sports?
- What if they're not gifted athletes?
- What if they're not first string!

These are all normal questions and concerns.

The everyday struggles we encounter in raising children can be compounded by unexpected changes in our lives and those of our children. If a child who has been developing normally and experiencing few difficulties suddenly starts to have problems, it may be related to changes in the child's environment.

It is not uncommon for a child who has been toilet trained to start wetting the bed again following a move or other event. The birth of a sibling may cause young children to regress because they're no longer the center of attention. Changing schools may be related to a drop in grades. The loss of a friend may cause a child to withdraw and even appear depressed. If you notice changes, consult your spouse and look for possible events that might have had a negative impact on your child's feelings.

Dramatic changes in behavior or functioning are easy to identify. Unfortunately, subtle changes that occur over a period of weeks, months, and sometimes years are less evident to parents and even to the children themselves. Kids' grades don't go from As to Fs in a week. Generally, there is a gradual decline that becomes evident only after a period of weeks or months.

Parents observe a child on a daily basis and most often compare behavior and functioning to the previous several days. It is only after reflection that a parent can recognize that something is now different for this child than it was three or six months ago.

Problems sneak up on parents, just like difficulties sneak up on you at work. Things are going well, but certain projects have not been finished or updated, and all of a sudden, you are in crisis mode dealing with a problem that could have been prevented.

It's no different with children, but much more complex. They're constantly changing and developing, bringing you new questions and challenges. All the while, you are attempting to maintain and strengthen your relationship with your spouse, perform at the highest level at work, and still be there for your children when they need you.

Being a parent is hard, probably the toughest job in the world. We have to deal with all the expectations placed upon us by society, by relatives and friends, and by our harshest critics, namely ourselves.

There is a constant barrage of questions when something goes wrong.

- You ask yourself, "Why didn't I do it another way? What am I doing wrong? Am I too harsh with them?"
- Grandma might chime in, "You're not doing it right. Why can't you just do it the way your father and I did?"
- From your sister you hear, "I can't believe you let him get away with that!"
- Your brother reminds you that "boys will be boys."

You will get lots of advice, both well-meaning and not so well-meaning, on how to do the job perfectly, not just good enough, but perfectly! We take some of the advice and reject some of it, and go on our merry way, but nothing seems to work.

Guess who gets the blame? Sometimes it is society, sometimes it's the school, and sometimes it's the parents, but mostly it is Mom. Moms are the guardians of the family's health and especially mental health. At times, mothers will get accolades, but more often they get blamed.

The expectation is that mothers will provide support for the family, feeding them, clothing them, nurturing them, and consoling them. They are expected to be experts in behavioral modification, human development, psychology, and counseling with no formal or informal training.

As dads, we shoulder some of the responsibility, but mostly it goes to Mom. It's extremely important for dads to understand that mothers not only have these external pressures placed upon them but also the internal pressures they place upon themselves.

The expectation for parenting perfection begins soon after the birth of a child. The positive attention from relatives soon wanes. The harsh reality of nighttime feedings, lack of sleep, dirty diapers, and demands of everyday life follows.

Because of the breakup of the extended family, moms and dads are left without support and direction. Questions they have about how to deal with a fussy baby, when to start feeding solids, normal childhood development, and other concerns are often left unanswered. This results in even more stress for the young mother and father. They are trying to become a team, but they don't have a coach. Where is the playbook?

The stresses of parenthood are further compounded as the child grows older and develops behavior problems. Mothers tend to recognize something is wrong much earlier than dads. Dads are more concerned about work and providing for the family. Often, it takes a crisis to bring Dad into the picture.

Prior to this, Mom has consulted friends, family, religious leaders, and even the family physician. Something is wrong, but she can't put her finger on it. Where is the troubleshooting section in the operating instructions?

Mom may begin to wonder if her child has a psychiatric condition. It's a concern that grows over time. It's not like one day a child wakes up and is out of control. As a child grows, worries arise.

- Jim is having a problem paying attention at school, and he is so hyper.
- Julie is so shy, and it seems like she's anxious all the time.
- George's temper tantrums just won't go away, and the last one went on for an hour.
- Janet seems so sad, and if you look at her the wrong way, she cries.
- Bill won't do what I say; he's always talking back.
- Jack is such a perfectionist; he has to have everything just so.
- My wife's ex was abusive, and now Joey is having such bad dreams he has to sleep with us. Is that okay?
- Sara is so panicky for no reason. Can kids have panic attacks?
- Jeannie stays out late, and those friends of hers are so weird. Oh no, do you think she's involved with drugs?

These questions leave parents at a loss.

Mothers seem to have a sixth sense about the fact that their children may have troubles, but at times they are afraid to bring this up to their spouses. They may feel their inability to solve these "simple problems" opens them up to even more criticism. They don't want to hear, "It's all your fault. If only you were a better mother." They condemn themselves enough; they don't need someone else to do it and reinforce their self-doubt. *Maybe it's just a stage? Maybe it's just normal, and I don't know the difference? Am I going to be labeled an overanxious mother?*

Guys, when your spouse comes to you with these problems, listen and listen carefully. Women are much more attuned to mental health issues in the family, and they need our support, not our criticism. Dads in general want to ignore a problem or at least minimize it. This is a bad mistake! Just because you feel uncomfortable dealing with emotions and especially with mental health concerns, **do not ignore** the problem.

TIME-OUT!

As a mental health professional, I recognize how difficult it is to seek psychiatric care for a child. A parent may be reluctant and think, *Is my child going to be labeled?* An underlying thought could be, *I really don't want to know if something is wrong. Maybe it will go away.*

Confronting reality is hard. It's easier to look the other way. But parents need help that does not intimidate them. They need a way to help them objectively screen for mental health problems before seeing a professional—a checklist they can fill out in the privacy of their own homes. Then they can decide for themselves if they should call a health-care provider for assistance.

For that reason, I have developed a screening tool consisting of forms that you are able to download online at no cost from www.freementalhealthscreening.com. The forms are designed to assist parents in evaluating their child's troubling symptoms. The Web site is very user-friendly. Everything is self-explanatory.

Your first stop should be the "Quick Screen." You can download and fill it out to assess the possibility of whether or not your child has a psychiatric condition. It's a guide to determine if there might be a problem. If you believe there is a problematic area, you may want to complete the more extensive comprehensive history and questionnaires. Parents can fill out the forms without the assistance of a professional.

The forms take about an hour to complete. It is important to note that the completed questionnaires do not give you a *diagnosis*. They do provide you with much of the information that professionals need to make a proper diagnosis. By taking an hour of your time and being prepared before visiting your clinician, you can give your child the best chance for proper care. You gain more control over the diagnostic process and become an integral part of the treatment team.

If, after you complete the forms, you don't think there is a problem, the information you have compiled can still be valuable. As we know with other medical tests, having a baseline becomes important for comparison should future concerns occur. In that instance, you will have a baseline of behaviors and symptoms for your child.

If you do decide to go to a clinician, your next step is to take these forms with you to your appointment. But remember, you wouldn't have your car towed to the mechanic, with a note taped to the windshield saying "fix it." No, you would give the auto professional as much information as possible about the problem. It makes the job easier and quicker and costs you less money in the long run. It means fewer tests and man-hours, making it a more efficient and timesaving process. It's the same when you go to a health professional. If you can give him or her all the information up front in an organized format, you will get better care. Guaranteed.

Even if none of your children has a problem, it can be helpful if you go to the Web site and fill out the forms for each one of them. These are documents for future reference throughout their lives. They will have a history of the pregnancy and documentation of any developmental problems they may have experienced as youngsters. A history of any early behavioral difficulties, speech problems, or history of abuse is included. Their academic performance from kindergarten through high school and any stressors they may have experienced during childhood and adolescence will be recorded. If they have received treatment for any mental health condition, they will have documentation of the counseling they received and the medications that were prescribed.

We now know that many psychiatric conditions have a hereditary component and can be passed from one generation to the next. For that reason, a complete family history is essential for appropriate diagnosis and treatment of psychiatric problems. Depression, bipolar disorder, anxiety and panic disorders, substance abuse conditions, and attention deficit hyperactivity disorder are examples of hereditary psychiatric conditions. These conditions are not unlike other medical problems such as diabetes that tend to run in families. If your primary care doctor asks about high blood pressure, cancer, diabetes, or other medical conditions in your family, you do not think twice about giving him or her that information.

Psychiatric illnesses are often hidden, even from close family members, because of the stigma that continues to be associated with mental health problems. It is important for you as a parent to ask the difficult questions of your relatives in order to obtain a complete and thorough psychiatric history to pass on to your children.

Generally, children react to stress in their lives by behaving differently. A five-year-old will not tell you verbally that he or she is upset. If there is significant conflict in the home with constant fighting and bickering between parents, a five-year-old may begin having conflicts with peers or difficulty sleeping. Children this age may feel they are the cause of the parental conflict. They begin to think negatively about themselves and demonstrate their low self-esteem through poor performance in school or other areas of their lives.

Parents may bring children into a conflict and in some instances even subtly ask them to choose sides. Children placed in these situations act out their frustrations. Parents have difficulties identifying these acting-out behaviors as a cry for help and understanding. They may personalize the issue and think they're being made the scapegoat. *Johnny is acting up just to make my life miserable. If my spouse would just handle Susie differently, we wouldn't have these problems.* When there is conflict in the home, parents need to reflect on their own behaviors. Counseling for the couple and their child may be indicated in this situation.

It is beyond the scope of this book to deal in depth with the psychiatric or mental health conditions that may become evident in childhood or adolescence. It is important to understand that all mental health conditions are present on a continuum. Psychiatric illnesses are no different than other medical conditions.

Diabetes, for example, may present in various forms and degrees of severity. Individuals may develop mildly elevated blood sugar levels if they become overweight and have a family history of diabetes. If they're good role models for their children, they will begin exercising and place themselves on a diet low in carbohydrates, and the problem will go away. Their brother or sister may not be so fortunate and, in spite of appropriate exercise and diet, have blood sugar levels that remain high. They may need to take oral medication to bring their blood sugar levels back to normal. Exercise and diet remain an important part of treating their condition but are not sufficient to control the illness.

Other family members may have developed diabetes as a child or adolescent. They may require insulin shots to treat their condition. They have the most severe form of the illness. All inherited the tendency to become diabetic, but the illness showed itself differently in each individual in the family. It is no different with psychiatric illnesses. The severity of illness may vary from person to person, and each person in a family will have an individual predisposition to develop a psychiatric condition.

Environmental factors impact all medical illnesses to some degree. Stress appears to be important in the development of psychiatric problems. Most psychiatric conditions have their onset following some type of emotionally stressful event. The stress response in our bodies tends to trigger changes in our brains, which cause the symptoms of various psychiatric illnesses. A genetic predisposition to develop a certain condition appears to determine whether or not any one individual will manifest evidence of that particular mental illness. Combat is a good example of severe psychological and physical stress. Although all of the men in a particular combat unit may experience similar stress, only a percentage will develop post-traumatic stress disorder (PTSD).

The same thing occurs in families. One child may develop a psychiatric problem, whereas brothers and sisters living in the same family will experience no difficulty. Although genetics may be the most significant determining factor, each child in the family experiences stresses at different times in their development. We now know that there are critical periods in a child's life when stress may impact development more strongly. For example, parents divorcing and the upheaval associated with this event may affect a three-year-old more than a teenager who is about to graduate from high school.

Understanding that psychiatric symptoms may present on a continuum from mild to severe is important in assessing the need for treatment. Minimal symptoms may respond to behavioral intervention or counseling, whereas more severe symptoms may require medications. Since psychiatric conditions involve behavior, almost all will benefit from counseling to some degree. Most mental health professionals would recommend counseling in combination with medications for even the most severe psychiatric problems. You can't go wrong by starting counseling for you and your child if there is a problem. It is important, however, to understand that medications can be lifesaving in some situations.

Using the forms at www.freementalhealthscreening.com will help you assess the presence of a particular psychiatric condition and also the severity of symptoms your child is manifesting. This can help you in making a determination as to whether you need to look beyond counseling and consider an evaluation by a professional who can prescribe medications.

If there is a family history of a particular mental health problem, you should seek an evaluation by a professional who can prescribe medications. It does not necessarily mean that your child will require intervention with medications, but it gives you the option earlier in the evaluation process. For example, if you or your spouse has a history of attention deficit hyperactivity disorder (ADHD) treated with medication and there are several other relatives with that condition in the extended family, it is more likely your child with ADHD will require medication. It might be best in this situation to see a medical professional initially. Behavioral interventions are important but may not be sufficient to fully treat a condition.

The conditions that parents may encounter in their children that might require medications are: attention deficit hyperactivity disorder, anxiety and panic disorders, depression, and bipolar disorder. I will describe each of these briefly. Should you suspect your child has any one of these conditions, you should consult your health professional after filling out the forms on the Free Mental Health Screening Web site. There are several other psychiatric conditions such as autism, Asperger's syndrome, and other fairly rare conditions that will not be included but can cause significant difficulties for children and their families. Space does not allow discussion of all the conditions, but there are many good Web sites that can provide information.

Attention Deficit Hyperactivity Disorder

Attention deficit hyperactivity disorder (ADHD) is a condition found in approximately 5 to 7 percent of children and adolescents in the United States. There are three forms of ADHD.

The *hyperactive-impulsive type* is found more frequently in boys. These children have to be on the go and may be unable to remain seated even during dinner. They are extremely fidgety and are often up and out of their seats in a school environment. These kids blurt out answers in class and will often interrupt others' conversations. Parents will tell me, "Johnny never walked; he ran from the very beginning." These children generally are identified when they reach school age because of their disruptive behavior in a classroom setting.

The *inattentive type* of ADHD is less evident to parents until they receive a report from school that their child is not performing up to potential. These children often have difficulty focusing and experience problems completing their work. They are likely to forget the books they need for a homework assignment at school. If they remember to bring the books home and you help them with an assignment, they may forget to turn it in the next day. They are less likely to be identified early since they are not disruptive in the classroom. The quiet child in the back of the room does not receive much attention from the teacher. They're often overlooked but suffer greatly because of their condition.

The most frequently diagnosed *combination type* has both the hyperactive-impulsivity and inattentive symptoms. These children not only have difficulty with overactivity and impulsive behaviors but the inattentive symptoms of problems with organization, making careless mistakes, and not completing tasks.

Children with ADHD are very frustrating for parents. You might tell them to take out the trash, clean their room, and start working on their homework. Thirty minutes later, you find that they were able to get the trash to the garbage can but were distracted by the dog in the backyard and did not make it back into the house. Children with ADHD require structure, structure, and more structure. They require written lists to help them remember chores and homework and then a list to remember the list.

Previously, we thought ADHD magically disappeared when teenagers turned eighteen. We now know this is not the case. This condition can have a profound impact on daily functioning for adults as well as children and adolescents. The World Health Organization interviewed two hundred thousand adults in thirty countries and determined that 3.5 percent of those interviewed had ADHD. The rate in the United States was 4.5 percent.

One research study evaluated seven thousand employed workers between the ages of eighteen and forty-four.[161] The researchers found that those individuals with ADHD missed work twenty-two days per year more than those without the condition. The ADHD group experienced another twenty-two days with reduced productivity and had fourteen days of reduced quality of their work.

The study found that ADHD caused more problems than depression. ADHD was felt to be more severely debilitating than many other psychiatric disorders and accounted for more accidents, more sick days, and more problems interacting with coworkers.

ADHD is a very treatable condition. Milder forms of the condition may respond to counseling and behavioral interventions. Moderate to severe forms generally require medication, which can produce dramatic results. Parents may observe significant improvement in school performance with grades going from Ds and Cs to As and Bs in a matter of weeks. Unfortunately, the condition often goes unrecognized and can result in years of frustration and failure.

I recall a man in his late thirties who came for treatment. He had recently been divorced by his wife, had lost his second business, and was experiencing an overwhelming sense of failure. He always had difficulties paying attention in school, and his difficulty organizing and following through on the job site had cost him dearly. He was started on medication to treat his ADHD and noticed a dramatic improvement in his capacity to function on the job and socially with those around him. When he was asked about the benefits of the treatment, he said, "If I had been diagnosed and treated earlier, I would not have lost my business and my family." (Attention deficit hyperactivity disorder is assessed on page three of the questionnaires found at www.freementalhealthscreening.com.)

Anxiety

Anxiety is a symptom we all experience. We might become anxious about an upcoming job interview or an important presentation we have to give at work. We may be nervous about jumping off the high dive for the first time or going down a black diamond ski run. These are normal apprehensions. Severe anxiety, however, can be debilitating and paralyzing.

People with panic attacks often will show up at the emergency room thinking they're having a heart attack. They have trouble breathing, their hearts are racing, they're sweating, and they feel like they're going to die. Children can develop panic attacks, and it can be frightening for both them and their parents. The anxious, shy child often suffers in silence since he or she does not act out like the hyperactivity ADHD child.

Some children can also develop obsessive compulsive disorder, which can cause great difficulties in life. These children often are obsessed with cleanliness and the need for sameness in their lives. Some parents might not mind having children who insist on their rooms being in perfect order. But I'm sure they would not like the tantrums these children throw if just one toy is out of place or a book is out of order on the shelf.

There are medications that can be of assistance in treating children with anxiety disorders; however, counseling and behavioral intervention should be tried initially in most cases. (Anxiety disorders are assessed on page seven of the questionnaires found at www.freementalhealthscreening.com.)

Depression

Depression is an illness that occurs all too frequently in children and adolescents. We want our children to be happy, and at times, we have difficulty understanding that they might be suffering without our knowledge. Some children will manifest their depression through anger and irritability. This can be confusing for parents. These children will experience problems with sleep, appetite, attention, and concentration. They have feelings of worthlessness. When asked, they may talk about feeling hopeless, feeling helpless to change their condition, and being suicidal. No parents want to hear this from their children, but the questions need to be posed.

If you are seeing unexplained episodes of crying, irritability, anger, and withdrawal from friends and family, you might want to go to page one of the Parent Questionnaire at Free Mental Health Screening.com. It is important to have your child or adolescent fill out the corresponding portion of the Child or Adolescent Questionnaire to get a full picture of what he or she is experiencing. Children and adolescents may have difficulty talking about these issues but can report them quite accurately if they're given the opportunity, especially with a written questionnaire.

Unfortunately, the diagnosis and treatment of depression in children and adolescents has become controversial in the last several years. Some studies have indicated that there may have been an increase in suicidal thoughts for children and adolescents who had been started on antidepressant medications to treat their depression. There were no actual suicides reported in the studies; however, the Food and Drug Administration placed a black-box warning (an indication of a potentially fatal side effect) on the use of antidepressants for children and adolescents.

Since the black-box warning has been in place, there has been an increase in completed suicides for children and adolescents. It is felt that this increase may be a result of the decrease in prescribing medication for depression in this population. Medications are available to treat depression in children and adolescents. They should be considered if the depression is severe—especially if there is a family history of mood disturbance. Counseling is indicated in almost every situation in order to assist children in developing coping skills to deal with their illness and to help them with their self-esteem.

Bipolar Disorder

The controversy regarding bipolar disorder in children and adolescents continues to be problematic for children suffering from this condition. Since many of the bipolar symptoms overlap with those of ADHD, it can be difficult to distinguish one from the other. Some bipolar disorder authorities contend that 70 percent to 80 percent of children with bipolar disorder also suffer from ADHD. In my opinion, children and adolescents do develop bipolar disorder. In many cases, I find a family history of the disorder and/or relatives with a high level of mood disturbances, drug and alcohol problems, and depression.

Bipolar disorder, like anxiety disorders, depression, and ADHD, has a genetic component. Younger children with this condition may have a history of severe and prolonged temper tantrums sometimes lasting hours. They tend to be aggressive, to have no fear, and to be bold and outgoing, and yet are quite sensitive. They may have major difficulties with sleep and experience wide mood fluctuations.

Bipolar kids can be extremely oppositional and have significant difficulties interacting with peers. As they get older, they experience major problems in school, and many become involved with drugs and alcohol as teenagers. They have a combination of depressed mood and periods of feeling extremely good and invincible. If asked, they may admit to feeling "ten feet tall and bulletproof," or they may have outlandish plans or grandiose ideas. Their thoughts may race, and they may have episodes of talking very rapidly.

Young bipolar children will have rapid changes in their moods—sometimes four to five times a day. They can be very loving at one moment and out of control the next. This may be followed closely by a period of crying and utter despair.

Unfortunately, it is usually ten years from the onset of symptoms of bipolar disorder until it is correctly diagnosed and treated. It is very important to recognize and treat the condition early, because for every year that the disease goes untreated, there is a 10 percent lower likelihood of recovery.[162]

As a psychiatrist who treats adults as well as kids, I see patients in their forties and even fifties who have been suffering since early childhood with undiagnosed bipolar disorder. Their lives are in shambles. They have tried self-medication with drugs and alcohol, are unable to work, and are frequently on public assistance. What a waste, because, once diagnosed, bipolar disorder can be treated with good results. Medications are almost always indicated even for children, and counseling is equally important to assist the child and family in dealing with this difficult illness.

Elevated mood or manic symptoms can be found at the bottom of page seven of the Child and Adolescent Questionnaire at the Web site www.freementalhealthscreening.com. Depression symptoms of a bipolar condition are found on page one of the questionnaire.

INSTANT REPLAY

- Early recognition and treatment of mental disorders can allow both parents and children to live normal productive lives.
- Women are much more attuned to mental health issues in the family, and they need your support, not your criticism.
- Objectively screen for problems before seeing a professional by visiting the Web site www.freementalhealthscreening.com.

"The brook would lose its song if you remove the rocks." —Unknown[163]

"The world breaks everyone, and afterward many are stronger at the broken places." —Ernest Hemingway[164]

CHAPTER 14

SPIRITUALITY

The Importance of Attending Religious Services

"The Ten Commandments were not a suggestion."
–Pat Riley, former NBA player and head coach of five championship teams[165]

According to *UCLA basketball coach* John Wooden, "The worst thing about new books is that they keep us from reading the old ones." [166] He is absolutely correct in his statement. We often think that new is better, that if we are the first one on the block to talk about the latest fad, it somehow enhances our standing in the world. Being the first is wrongly equated with being the best. However, most of the time, we are more likely to succeed if we utilize the tried and true rather than the *new and untested*.

John Wooden knew that he needed to rely on something more meaningful than the latest book on "a half-court offense" or the "ultimate zone defense." He states in his book *Coach Wooden One-on-One* that he refers to the Bible for direction and solace on a daily basis. For him, "the old book" is a constant companion and the basis for his success in coaching and life. A great coach is always learning from other coaches, and Coach Wooden relied on the Greatest Coach of All.

"John Wooden taught us how to be the best we could be yet remain true to ourselves. Coach never asked us about our religion or our politics, but it was impossible not to know that he had an intensely strong and unshakable faith in God and that he drew upon the Bible for many of the principles by which he

lived. As a result, his sacrifice, patience, and devotion are the greatest examples and influences I have had in my life." —Bill Walton, NBA All Star, UCLA All American, and NBC basketball announcer[167]

"Coach Wooden is my friend and a great mentor. I've admired him as a coach and even more as a person. Other books have told us of his coaching accomplishments, but *Coach Wooden: One-on-One* lets us look at the person and his faith. Thanks, Coach, for being a great example." —Roy Williams, head basketball coach, University of North Carolina[168]

These are just a couple of the comments about Coach Wooden, which emphasize his reliance on religious teaching for guidance and support. Many of Coach Wooden's famous quotes are related directly to teachings from the Bible. He said, "Material possessions, winning scores, and great reputations are meaningless in the eyes of the Lord, because He knows what we really are and that is all that matters."[169] "The Bible tells us not to worry about earthly things but to be concerned about having faith and performing good works."[170]

It bears repeating that Coach Wooden emphasized the need to "consider the rights of others before your own rights."[171] The Bible repeatedly asks us to walk in the shoes of our friends and enemies and to set the example for forgiveness and caring. In John Wooden's words, "There are many things that are essential to arriving at true peace of mind, and one of the most important is faith, which cannot be acquired without prayer."[172] He set the example by praying daily and maintaining his faith through hardship and self-doubt.

> "When the world pushes you to your knees, you are in a perfect position to pray."[173] **—Islamic quote from Pearls of Wisdom**

Coach Wooden said, "Be prepared and be honest."[174] He summarized in just a few words the basis for living a moral and productive life. We all must be prepared to face life's challenges in a manner that will reflect well upon us, our

SPIRITUALITY

families, and our faith. In addition, we must be honest with ourselves, with our families, with everyone, and most especially with our God.

Red Auerbach, a Jewish coach who still holds the record for most consecutive National Basketball Association championship titles—eight with the Boston Celtics—demonstrated his concerns about living a moral and honest life when he said, "The only correct actions are those that demand no explanation and no apology."[175] He made history by drafting the first African-American basketball player in 1950 and starting five black NBA players in 1964.[176] He effectively broke down the color barrier in professional basketball. Sometimes actions do speak louder than words.

Throughout his writings, Coach Wooden emphasizes certain precepts that he has found useful as a coach, a father, and a person of faith. He stated, "The most important profession in the world is parenting. Parents are the first coaches a child has."[177] He used many of the principles he was taught as a child and that he gleaned from the Bible in his work with young athletes. Many times, he acted as a surrogate father to his young charges.

Coach Wooden writes about how he provided a supportive environment for his athletes and assistant coaches; how he always strived to be the example for his players to imitate (he even quit smoking); how he would set limits even if it meant benching his best player and losing the game; how he always emphasized his role as a teacher and the need for his players to complete their education; and how, by example, he demonstrated the importance of faith and spiritual well-being.

Coach Wooden used the principles of Support, Modeling for Imitation, Limits, Education, and Spirituality with great success. That is if you can define success by listing unequaled records as a college basketball coach, which include:

- eighty-eight consecutive victories, next best, sixty;
- ten NCAA championships, next best, four;
- seven consecutive NCAA championships, next best, two;
- thirty consecutive NCAA tournament victories, previous record, thirteen;
- four undefeated full seasons, next best, one; and
- ESPN's selection as the number-one greatest coach of all time.

Not bad for a guy who coached at UCLA for fifteen years before winning a national championship. Talk about perseverance, hard work, repetition, repetition, and more repetition. He stuck to the basics and had faith in himself, in his coaching staff, in his players, and most important, in God.

John Wooden is not the only coach to emphasize a spiritual component to his coaching and life. Vince Lombardi preached the importance of internalizing principles and values. "Faith was the basis of his discipline, and the respect instilled by his Jesuit teachers—for his teachers and for God—had a lasting impact on his attitude toward authority."[178] When speaking of the need for values in life he stated, "Improvements in moral character are our own responsibility. Bad habits are eliminated, not by others, but by ourselves."[179]

> *"Everybody should establish their own do-right benchmarks. If you have doubts concerning the difference between right or wrong, consult your Bible or Torah. You will find it's worth the effort."*
> **—Lou Holtz**[180]

When Coach Holtz was asked how to obtain the trust of others, he said, "The answer is surprisingly simple: just do right. Live an honorable life. Do what is right and avoid what is wrong."[181] I know I used this quote before, but it's all about repetition, repetition, repetition.

Lou Holtz was inducted into the football hall of fame in 2008. He is the only coach in NCAA history to lead six different college football programs into bowl games. By the way, he also led Notre Dame to a National Championship in 1988. So according to Lou, if it's morally and ethically right, just do it! If it's wrong, don't even think about it!

When it comes to parenting and striving to be the best dad possible, it's good to remember Coach Holtz's statement, "I can't believe that God put us on earth to be ordinary."[182] You can do it, because you have God's help and your religious teachings as a guide.

SPIRITUALITY

Successful coaches emphasize spirituality and the benefits of religion. Being spiritual and especially attending religious services has a dramatic effect on children's lives. Numerous scientific studies have demonstrated a direct correlation between religious upbringing and positive outcomes for the children and adolescents. This positive impact has the potential to influence their behavior over their lifetimes.

You don't get the benefit if you don't go to services, so here are some statistics about attendance and children. Attending religious services regularly during childhood was associated with a 61 percent probability of attending services as an adult. Those who did not attend as a child had only a 22 percent probability of attending later in their lives. Almost two-thirds of the parents who attended religious services as children take their own children to services regularly. Adults who had attended services as a child were 50 percent more likely to pray during the week.[183]

You might ask yourself why these statistics are important. How can going to religious services and participating in religious activities have a long-lasting effect on your children?

Researchers found that such behaviors can add eight years to children's life expectancies and significantly reduce their risks for problems with drugs and alcohol. Religious affiliation is associated with a dramatically lower risk for suicide and can help children and teens rebound from depression more easily. It can decrease the risk for rebellious behavior and decrease the likelihood of becoming involved in criminal activities.

Going to religious services regularly can improve children's attitudes about school and elevate their academic performances. Teens who regularly attend services are less likely to become sexually active at an early age and are more likely to wear seat belts. Religious involvement is associated with increased self-esteem and a greater satisfaction with life. It provides children with a lifelong, positive, altruistic outlook on life and the moral compass necessary for true success.

Another study looked at the relationship between mothers who attended religious services and the mental health and social functioning of their adolescent children.[184] In this particular study, the adolescents themselves may not have accompanied their mothers.

The children were eleven through thirteen years of age. Two-thirds were felt to be at risk for developing psychiatric problems, and one-third was thought unlikely to develop difficulties. Those mothers who attended regularly were more likely to come from an intact two-parent family. They had a better education, and their income was significantly higher.

Things that were not factors in the outcome of this study included race, the number of individuals in the household, the sex of the child, or the grade in school. Those children whose mothers participated regularly in religious activities reported greater satisfaction with their health, were more involved in their families, had greater skills in solving health-related problems, and felt greater support from their friends.

Another study surveyed almost nine thousand children and adolescents and eight thousand parents. It examined the relationship between religious involvement and the strength of family ties. The children from families who had the most involvement in religious activities tended to have better relationships with their parents. They participated more frequently in family activities and were less likely to run away from home. Greater participation in religious activities was associated with better overall outcomes for the children.

The same study found that mothers from the more religious families were strict but offered praise frequently. They were more likely to know their children's close friends and to know where their children were when they were away from home. Fathers also knew their children's close friends and the parents of their friends, and were familiar with their school experiences. The children from these homes were more likely to admire their fathers and to want to model themselves after them. The children felt their fathers were more supportive and less likely to disappoint them by canceling plans.

Was it that parents who emphasized the importance of religion in their family parented differently? Or was it that religion, faith, and spirituality had an impact on their parenting philosophy? The study could not answer these questions.

SPIRITUALITY

Does it make any difference? We're looking for results. The kids did better in families that emphasized a spiritual component to family life. If it works, do it!

Other studies had shown that religious teens were less likely to use drugs, smoke, or drink. They received fewer traffic tickets, tended to wear seat belts more frequently, and were less likely to be involved in risk taking. (Remember, the leading causes of death of adolescents are accidents, homicides, and suicides.) The teens who went to religious services went to bars less often, were less likely to get into fights, and did not engage as frequently in delinquent behaviors such as trespassing, arson, shoplifting, and other forms of stealing. Religious twelfth graders had better self-esteem and a more positive outlook on life. They exercised more, had fewer behavior problems in school, were less likely to be truant, and even argued less with their parents. If taking our children to services once a week can produce these kinds of results, where do we sign up?

Dr. Lynda Powell, a psychologist who was not a churchgoer and was skeptical about the influence of religion on health, was asked to head a three-scientist panel selected by the National Institute of Health to review literature "purporting to link religion to health." The panel did not find a positive relationship between religion and health once people became ill. However, when they examined healthy people who regularly attended religious services, they came to an entirely different conclusion.

Dr. Powell said, "After seeing the data, I think I should go to church." The panel found that for those who attended religious services regularly there was a 25 percent lower mortality rate. That means that for every one hundred deaths by non-attendees, there were only seventy-five deaths among those who attended.

The researchers felt there were a number of factors that may have resulted in fewer deaths for those regular attendees. The act of worshiping was felt to contribute to the differences. Those who worshiped were more likely to meditate; to have a set of moral values that discouraged excessive drinking, smoking, and carousing; and to have a supportive social network.[185]

Other researchers have also written about the importance of religion, spirituality, and altruism in the development of resilience. In the face of stress, adversity, trauma, or tragedy, "a resilient person is one who is able to bounce back from difficult experiences by adapting to life's changing demands."[186] It bears repeating that having a strong moral compass is a characteristic found in resilient individuals.

Developing and maintaining a framework of belief that few things can shatter is thought to enhance an individual's ability to find meaning in and cope adaptively with adversity. Having a spiritual outlook or religion can provide that framework of belief.

An analysis of forty-two different studies including 126,000 individuals has demonstrated a significant reduction in mortality rates for people involved in religious practice. Religious beliefs correlated with a lower rate of depression in numerous populations.

Elderly people living in the community, college students, individuals grieving the loss of a loved one, and medically ill older people who had stronger religious beliefs suffered less from depression. If people did become depressed, they recovered quicker if they had a higher level of religious involvement. Religious adolescents have lower suicide rates. Active involvement seems to be correlated with neurochemical changes in the brain. These brain changes may contribute to resilience and protect against the development of stress-related psychiatric illness.

An altruistic, helpful attitude toward others is another important component of the moral compass. Finding meaning in contributing to society and doing for others are important components of resilience. Having meaningful goals for life and work as well as a moral framework are all part of a resilient individual's composition.

The capacity to find meaning in tragedy and move forward towards a loftier goal helps people conquer adversity. Those who helped others during World War II bombing attacks were much less likely to suffer from trauma-induced mood and anxiety symptoms. Those individuals who had experienced emotional difficulties prior to the attacks noticed a decrease in their symptoms after they became involved in helping others.

We can see how teaching altruism to our children can help insulate them from psychological difficulties as they grow older. The moral seeds we plant today will produce a bountiful harvest of benefits not only for our children but for those around them as well.

SPIRITUALITY

Research has linked participation in religiously oriented programs with the development of a positive ethnic identity and the formation of relationships with positive role models. The development of positive skills related to work and school and a decrease in stress are associated with religious involvement.

Another study of almost one hundred thousand adolescents who were involved in religious activities showed that these teenagers had an increased number of developmental skills and were at a decreased risk for negative behaviors.

Teens who reported regular involvement in religious activities performed above average academically. A further study of approximately eight thousand youth demonstrated that when the children came from families who displayed high levels of nurturance, closeness, and affection plus regular involvement in religious activities the teens were less likely to use drugs and alcohol.

The protective effects of religious commitment were not due to any specific religious orientation "but rather to a strong religious commitment to basic life-preserving values, beliefs, and practices."[187]

In a study of 371 severely depressed participants, those with no religious affiliation were more likely to attempt suicide, to think about suicide more frequently, and to have relatives who had committed suicide. Individuals with religious affiliations were more likely to have a family-oriented social network and to spend more time with first-degree relatives. They were less likely to be aggressive and impulsive and to use alcohol or drugs. Those with strong religious connections were more likely to have had family responsibilities, child-related concerns, and moral objections to suicide as reasons for living.

The researchers concluded that "religious commitment promotes social ties and reduces alienation." The families of the religiously connected subjects were perceived to provide "reliable emotional support, nurturance, and reassurance of worth."[188]

The Annie E. Casey Foundation conducted research concerning the welfare of low-income children around the country. The U.S. government collects data measuring "a child's physical and mental health, education, team membership, family involvement, family structure, neighborhood, and income."

The study found that underprivileged children fared worst in some of the wealthiest states including Massachusetts, Rhode Island, New York, New Jersey, Maryland, and Delaware. The states where poor children fared the best were in the Rocky Mountain and Great Plains regions. The top five states were Utah, North Dakota, Idaho, Wyoming, and South Dakota. In general, children living in poverty scored low on twenty-seven of twenty-nine well-being indicators.

Poor children who scored as well or better than high-income kids were the ones who attended religious services weekly and ate dinner with their families six out of the seven days in a week. It's called family structure.

Although most of the studies cited in this book were based on attendance at Christian churches and Jewish synagogues, this does not diminish the importance of the structure and social support offered by other faiths.

INSTANT REPLAY

- The great coaches know the importance of moral principles.
- Religious involvement has a positive impact on children.
- Teens attending religious services are less likely to become involved with drugs and alcohol or have problems with the law.
- Parents who set the example by attending services have more satisfying family relationships.
- Families who worship together have stronger family ties.
- Families who have a religious affiliation are healthier and live longer.

SPIRITUALITY

Remember to implement the S-M-I-L-E-S program, work with and support your spouse, and take care of your physical, emotional, and spiritual needs. Do these things and you will have done everything in your power to prepare your child for life. You will be a "gold-medal" dad.

To help you on your journey, I offer an Irish blessing.

May the road rise to meet you.

May the wind be always at your back.

May the sun shine warm upon your face,

The rains fall soft upon your fields, and

Until we meet again,

May God hold you in the palm of His hand.

"Train the child in the way he should go, and when he is old, he will not turn from it." —Proverbs 22:6

ENDNOTES

---

1. Retrieved from Quote, http://www.brainyquote.com.

2. Ibid.

3. Ibid.

4. Ibid.

5. Eamon Brown, *1001 Motivational Messages and Quotes: Teaching Character Through Sports* (Monterey, CA: Coaches Choice, 2001).

6. Ibid.

7. Ibid.

8. "War Comes Home for Mother-Soldiers in Iraq," *NPR Morning Edition*, Nov. 13, 2007.

9. Jiongjiong Wang, PhD, "Gender Difference in Neural Response to Psychological Stress," Medscape from WebMD. Posted Nov. 5, 2007, http://www.www.medscape.com/viewarticle/563705.

10. Brown, *1001 Motivational Messages and Quotes*.

11. Ibid.

12. Jeff Janssen, MS, and Greg Dale, PhD, *The Seven Secrets of Successful Coaches: How to Unlock and Unleash Your Team's Full Potential* (Cary, NC: Winning the Mental Game, 2006).

13. Brainy Quote.

14. Janssen and Dale, *The Seven Secrets of Successful Coaches*, .

15. Ibid.

16. Ibid., 137.

17. Lou Holtz, *Winning Every Day: The Game Plan for Success* (New York: Harper Business, 1998), 123.

18. Ibid., 194.

19. Ibid., 194.

20. Ibid., 195.

21. Janssen and Dale, *The Seven Secrets of Successful Coaches*, 17.

22. Brainy Quote.

23. Holtz, *Winning Every Day*, 186.

24. Ibid., 187.

25. Ibid., 194.

26. John Wooden and Jay Carty, *Coach Wooden One-on-One: Inspiring Conversations on Purpose, Passion and the Pursuit of Success* (Ventura, CA: Regal Books, 2003).

27. Wooden and Carty, *Coach Wooden One-on-One*.

28. Brainy Quote.

29. Ibid.

30. Wooden and Carty, *Coach Wooden One-on-One*.

31. Brainy Quote.

32. Vince Lombardi, Jr., *The Lombardi Rules: 26 Lessons from Vince Lombardi the World's Greatest Coach* (New York: McGraw Hill, 2005), 6.

Endnotes

33. Lombardi, *The Lombardi Rules*, 78.

34. Brainy Quote.

35. Janssen and Dale, *The Seven Secrets of Successful Coaches*.

36. Lombardi, *The Lombardi Rules*, 19.

37. Holtz, *Winning Every Day*.

38. Ibid.

39. Janssen and Dale, *The Seven Secrets of Successful Coaches*.

40. Holtz, *Winning Every Day*.

41. Wooden and Carty, *Coach Wooden One-on-One*.

42. Janssen and Dale, *The Seven Secrets of Successful Coaches*.

43. Ibid.

44. Holtz, *Winning Every Day*.

45. Wooden and Carty, *Coach Wooden One-on-One*.

46. Janssen and Dale, *The Seven Secrets of Successful Coaches*, 15.

47. Brown, *1001 Motivational Messages and Quotes*.

48. Ibid.

49. Lombardi, *The Lombardi Rules*, 79.

50. Brainy Quote.

51. Holtz, *Winning Every Day*.

52. Ibid., 182–183.

53. Wooden and Carty, *Coach Wooden One-on-One*, 16.

54. bbBrainy Quote.

55. Wooden and Carty, *Coach Wooden One-on-One*, 21.

56. Holtz, *Winning Every Day*, 128.

57. Lombardi, *The Lombardi Rules*, 27.

58. Holtz, *Winning Every Day*, 154.

59. Brainy Quote.

60. Ibid.

61. Ibid.

62. Holtz, *Winning Every Day*.

63. Ibid.

64. Brainy Quote.

65. Holtz, *Winning Every Day*.

66. Nicole Cooper et al., "Resilience and Vulnerability to Trauma: Psychobiological Mechanisms," *Adolescent Psychopathology and the Developing Brain* (New York: Oxford University Press, 2007).

67. Holtz, *Winning Every Day*.

68. Brainy Quote.

69. Holtz, *Winning Every Day*.

70. Wooden and Carty, *Coach Wooden One-on-One*.

71. Brainy Quote.

Endnotes

72. Holtz, *Winning Every Day*.

73. Janssen and Dale, *The Seven Secrets of Successful Coaches*.

74. *Idaho Statesman*, Jan. 1, 2008.

75. Ibid.

76. Bill Christeson et al. "School or the Streets," *Fight Crime: Invest in Kids*(Lansing MI: 2008). Retrieved from http://www.fightcrime.org.

77. *Church of England Newspaper* (Sep. 4, 2008). Retrieved from www churchnewspaper.com.

78. Ibid.

79. Sexuality, Information, and Education Council of the United States. Retrieved from http://www.thebody.com/content/art2406.html.

80. Shahid Athar, "Where do we go from here?" Retrieved from themodernreligion.com.

81. Jane Ulman, "Jewish Ethics Should be Part of Sex Education for Children," *Jewish Telegraphic Agency*. Retrieved from http://www.jta.org/cgi-bin/iowa/news/article/19990923Jewishethicsshould.html.

82. Sarah L. Ashby, MD, MS, et al., **"Television Viewing and Risk of Sexual Initiation by Young Adolescents,"** *Archives of Pediatric and Adolescent Medicine* 160:4 (Apr. 4, 2006).

83. Wooden and Carty, *Coach Wooden One-on-One*.

84. Brainy Quote.

85. Ibid.

86. W. Maziak et al., "Childhood Obesity: Are We Missing the Big Picture?" *Obesity Reviews*9:1 (Apr. 16, 2007): 35–42.

87. *TIME* (June 23, 2008).

88. "Principal Says Banning Sugar Made Students Smarter" FOX News (Jan. 29, 2009).

89. Ibid.

90. David S. Ludwig, MD, PhD, "Obesity — The Shape of Things to Come," *New England Journal of Medicine* (Dec. 6, 2007).

91. "Fasting? It's good for your heart," *Lifestyle*, TV Network (Nov. 7, 2007).

92. Brainy Quote.

93. Ibid.

94. Crina Frincu-Mallos, "Caloric Intake Negatively Influences Sleep Patterns in Healthy Adults," *Medscape Psychiatry and Mental Health Medical News* (June 2008). Retrieved from http://www.medscape.com.

95. Brainy Quote.

96. Lori Oliwenstein, "Weighty Issues," *TIME* (Jun. 23, 2008).

97. Ibid.

98. Brainy Quote.

99. Ibid

100. Mayo Clinic Web site, "Fitness for Kids: Getting your Children Off the Couch" (Jan. 26, 2007). from http://www.mayoclinic.com.

101. Kid's Health Web site, http://kidshealth.org/kid.

102. *TIME* (June 23, 2008).

103. Brainy Quote.

104. Mayo Clinic Web site, "Exercise: 7 Benefits of Regular Physical Activity" (Jul. 26, 2007). Retrieved from http://www.mayoclinic.com.

105. Kathleen Kingsbury, "Fit at Any Size," *TIME* (Jun. 23, 2008).

106. Joyce Giammattei, PhD, "Television Watching and Soft Drink Consumption," *Archives of Pediatric and Adolescent Medicine* 157 (Sep. 2003).

107. Leonard Epstein, PhD, "A Randomized Trial of the Effects of Reducing Television Viewing and Computer Use on Body Mass Index in Young Children," *Archives of Pediatric and Adolescent Medicine* 162:3 (Mar. 3, 2008).

108. Elizabeth A. Vandewater, PhD, and Xuan Huang, MA, "Parental Weight Status as a Moderator of the Relationship Between Television Viewing and Childhood Overweight," *Archives of Pediatric and Adolescent Medicine* 160:4 (Apr. 4, 2006).

109. Andreas Loft, MD, et al., "Treadmill Exercise Activates Subcortical Neural Networks and Improves Walking after Stroke: A Randomized Controlled Trial," *Stroke* (Aug. 28, 2008). Retrieved from http://www.ncbi.nlm.nih.gov.

110. Brown, *1001 Motivational Messages and Quotes*.

111. Quote Garden, http://www.quotegarden.com/success.html.

112. Janssen and Dale, *The Seven Secrets of Successful Coaches*.

113. Ibid.

114. Brainy Quote.

115. Lombardi, *The Lombardi Rules*, 6–7.

116. Ibid., 15.

117. Holtz, *Winning Every Day*.

118. Becca Levy, "To Live Longer, Accentuate the Positive," *Psychiatric News* 37:18 (Sep. 20, 2002): 22.

119. "Serotonin Paucity May Predict Pessimism In Depression," *Psychiatric News* 38:2 (Jan. 17, 2003): 34.

120. Mayo Clinic Web site, "Tools For Healthier Lives, Positive-Thinking: Practice This Stress Management Skill." Retrieved from mayoclinic.com.

121. Ibid.

122. Brainy Quote.

123. Ibid.

124. James E Loehr, EdD, *Mental Toughness Training for Sports: Achieving Athletic Excellence* (Jan. 1986).

125. Brainy Quote.

126. Ibid.

127. Ibid.

128. Ibid.

129. Ibid.

130. Holtz, *Winning Every Day*.

131. Amanda Rose, PhD, "Co-Rumination in the Friendships of Girls and Boys," *Child Development* 73:6 (Nov.–Dec. 2002).

132. Melissa Dahl, "Quit Complaining—It May Make You Feel Worse," MSNBC (Aug. 13, 2007).

133. Denise Foley, "The Power of Pluck," *Prevention Magazine* (Dec. 4, 2007).

134. Steven Wolin, MD, and Sybil Wolin, *The Resilient Self: How Survivors of Troubled Families Rise Above Adversity* (Villard: Mar. 16, 1993).

135. Brainy Quote.

136. Holtz, *Winning Every Day.*

137. Brainy Quote.

138. Ibid.

139. Holtz, *Winning Every Day.*

140. Brainy Quote.

141. Masten, Ann S. "Children Who Overcome Adversity to Succeed in Life." University of Minnesota Extension Web site. 2000. <http://www.extension.umn.edu>

142. Jerrold F Rosenbaum, MD, and Jennifer M. Covino, MPA, "Stress and Resilience: Implications for Depression and Anxiety," *Medscape Psychiatry and Mental Health* (Oct. 2, 2005).

143. Daniel Romer and Elaine F. Walker, eds., *Adolescent Psychopathology and the Developing Brain: Integrating Brain and Prevention Science* (Oxford University Press, Feb. 2007).

144. **Fatih Ozbay, MD, et al.,** "Social Support and Resilience to Stress: From Neurobiology to Clinical Practice,"*Psychiatry* 4:5 (May 2007).

145. Ibid.

146. Walter R. Bixby et al., **"The Unique Relation of Physical Activity to Executive Function in Older Men and Women,"** *Medicine & Science in Sports & Exercise* 39:8 (Aug. 2007).

147. Brown, *1001 Motivational Messages and Quotes.*

148. Brainy Quote.

149. Ibid.

150. Madeline Vann, "Happy Marriage Eases Wife's Workday Tensions," *MSN Lifestyles* (Jan. 1, 2008).

151. Brainy Quote.

152. Ibid.

153. Brown, *1001 Motivational Messages and Quotes*.

154. Brainy Quote.

155. Ibid.

156. Ibid.

157. Ibid.

158. Brown, *1001 Motivational Messages and Quotes*.

159. Ronald C. Kessler, PhD, et al., "Lifetime Prevalence and Age-of-Onset Distributions of DSM-IV Disorders in the National Comorbidity Survey Replication," *Archives of General Psychiatry* (Jun. 2005).

160. Tracy Magee, PhD, and Sister Callista Roy, PhD, "School-Age Behavior Problems: The Role of Early Childhood Risk Factors," *Pediatric Nursing* 34:1 (2008).

161. Ron Kessler, "Adults With ADHD Lose 3 Weeks Worth of Work Annually," healthday.com (May 28, 2008). Retrieved from http://www.nlm.nih.gov.

162. **Tanvir Singh, MD**, "Pediatric Bipolar Disorder: Diagnostic Challenges in Identifying Symptoms and Course of Illness," *Psychiatry* 5:6 (Jun. 2008).

163. Brown, *1001 Motivational Messages and Quotes*.

164. Brainy Quotes.

165. Ibid.

166. Wooden and Carty, *Coach Wooden One-on-One*.

167. Ibid.

168. Ibid.

169. Ibid.

170. Ibid.

171. Brainy Quote.

172. Ibid.

173. Pearls of Wisdom: Islamic quotes. Retrieved from http://www.geocities.com/mutmainaa/pearls.html.

174. Brainy Quote.

175. Ibid.

176. Retrieved from http://encarta.msn.com.

177. Wooden and Carty, *Coach Wooden One-on-One*.

178. Lombardi, *The Lombardi Rules*, 78.

179. Ibid., 19.

180. Holtz, *Winning Every Day*.

181. Ibid.

182. Ibid.

183. Neil MacQueen, "Too Good to Be True (but it is): The Life Benefits of Regular Church Attendance." Retrieved from ://www.sundaysoftware.com/stats.htm.

184. Stuart R. Varon, MD, and Anne W. Riley, PhD, "The Relationship Between Maternal Church Attendance and Adolescent Mental Health and Social Functioning," *Psychiatric Services* (Jun. 1999).

185. Lynda K. Powell, PhD, "Religion and Spirituality: Linkages to Physical Health," *American Psychologist* 58(1) (Jan. 2003).

186. Romer and Walker, eds., Nicole S. Cooper et al., "Resilience and Vulnerability to Trauma Psychological Mechanisms in Adolescent Psychopathology and the Developing Brain."

187. Kanita Dervic, MD, "Religious Affiliation and Suicide Attempt," *Am J Psychiatry* 161 (Dec. 2004).

188. Ibid.

Printed in the USA
CPSIA information can be obtained
at www.ICGtesting.com
LVHW010822060424
776638LV00033B/1054